Katherine Ruonala is a mighty, anointed woman of God with a humble heart who has learned the key to moving in the supernatural. Her transparency as she takes you through her experiences and relationship with the Lord points to her sincerity and love for Jesus and His people. *Living in the Miraculous* is filled with powerful testimonies of healings, signs, and wonders that generate an insatiable yearning to cry out, "Use me, God!" If you have a hunger to heal the sick, a desire to move in miracles, a passion to see people set free, then this is a must-read book!

—Dr. Ché Ahn
Senior pastor, HROCK Church, Pasadena, California
President, Harvest International Ministry
International chancellor, Wagner Leadership Institute

In her book *Living in the Miraculous* Katherine Ruonala has brought forth a gem for the body of Christ. She writes not as an armchair theologian but as an experienced practitioner in the field. It has been many, many years since I have personally witnessed such a pure healing anointing on a woman's life. It is a sign to us of the great work God is doing in the earth today to make His fame known through signs and wonders. I highly commend to you the writings, the life, and the ministry of my dear friend and co-laborer in Christ Jesus, Katherine Ruonala.

—Dr. James W. Goll
Director, Encounters Network,
Prayer Storm, and Compassion Acts

For years Katherine Ruonala has not only walked in the miraculous, but she has also raised up a whole church full of young people who walk in the miraculous with her. Every week her church sends people to the streets, to the hospitals, to wherever the Holy Spirit leads them, in order to demonstrate the healing power of Jesus's love. As you read this book, you will discover how easy it is to enter into revival simply by listening to God's voice and doing what He says. We highly recommend it!

—WESLEY AND STACEY CAMPBELL
Senior pastors, New Life Church,
Kelowna, British Columbia
Founders, Be a Hero

The moment I met Katherine for the first time in Brisbane, Australia, I fell in love with her obvious passion and love for the Lord, His kingdom, and His righteousness. Her faith and zeal were infectious, and I loved hearing the glorious testimonies of the works of Christ through her ministry. It was not a surprise to me that Katherine chose to write *Living in the Miraculous*. She lives this message, and her generous spirit desires every believer to feast on the same revelations and glory she has discovered in Christ. I am confident that your faith thermometer will rise like never before after you read this wonderful book. And when it does, go and create waves for Him. You are a revival looking for a place to happen!

—PATRICIA KING
Founder, XPministries, and cofounder, XPmedia

Once you have met Katherine Ruonala, you will never forget her fresh, infectious passion and love for God. She doesn't just have a message—she lives the message! *Living in the Miraculous* is a book filled with many faith-building testimonies of the wonderful healing power of Jesus. It challenges us to expect the miraculous in everyday life and calls us higher to live a powerful life in the Spirit. This book describes Katherine's personal journey to discover her own identity in Christ and her passionate desire to live a supernatural life. *Living in the Miraculous* will inspire, challenge, and equip! It is a "must" for those who believe that presence and mission are inextricably linked.

—MARK MUMFORD
Salt and Light Ministries
United Kingdom

From the Great Southland of the Holy Spirit, mighty revivalists are coming forth. Healing, salvation, and power from on high characterize their ministries. Katherine Ruonala is one who is leading the charge! She carries the favor of the Father and the love of Jesus wherever she goes. *Living in the Miraculous* will change your life. The testimony of Jesus drips from every page. Katherine's amazing life story and the works of glory that accompany her ministry seem to pour off the pages of this book into the reader.

Katherine is a friend of the Holy Spirit. She has made it her life's ambition to walk as close to God as possible and for her life to be infused with the love of God. Within this book you will see your identity as Jesus's beloved partner, one who has unlimited grace to do the works of Jesus. This amazing book will make it possible for you to walk in the miraculous. Katherine gives you an entryway into the supernatural flow of God's life.

Everyone wants to experience miracles, but so few will

pay the price necessary to walk in the miraculous. Katherine has paid the price to be a carrier of the glory of God. Take this book with you, read it over thoroughly, and process the revelation she shares. Then you must take up the challenge yourself to walk in the faith-filled ways of miracle living. You can expect your heart to burn as you read it. Enjoy it, my friend! This is the time for God to break through and take you into supernatural living!

—Dr. Brian Simmons
Author and translator, *The Passion Translation*

Living in the Miraculous will transform you. It is much more than a book on the supernatural. It will change your way of living!

How can I be so sure? Katherine Ruonala's supernatural, miraculous lifestyle has done that for me. Her intimacy with Father God is so contagious that it greatly impacted me when we first met. Everything you read here she lives. It won't be long until you are experiencing that as well.

In *Living in the Miraculous* Katherine shares the joyful essence of how to supernaturally encounter and live in God's love in everyday life. As you read about Katherine's own walk of discovering the miraculous, you will discover this part of God's heart for you too! One of the things I love most about Katherine is that she freely helps others learn and live what she has experienced—and then you will begin to freely do that for others too!

So get ready for a glorious God encounter! You won't ever be the same again!

—Bruce Lindley
ARC Ministries

Within an hour of meeting Katherine I had personally been renewed and enthused with God's love and power. As I read this book, exactly the same thing happened. Through her life and through her writing people are being positioned to receive the life-transforming love and power of Christ. If you want to learn to live in a new level of grace and anointing and see the world around you changed, read this book and become a vessel of God's miracle-working love and power. I warmly commend it to you.

—ANDY BARCLAY-WATT
Senior leader, LifeChurch
Manchester, England

I felt increasingly drawn to the Father as I read this book. From her own firsthand experience, Katherine powerfully imparts the extravagant grace and unconditional love of God. You will be inspired by the triumph of God's healing power and the generosity of His revelation. The stunning authority that has been bestowed on us will challenge any religious mind-set. You will be greatly encouraged to understand how God's faithfulness more than bridges the gap of our humanity, making the impossible possible. A delightful, inspiring, and comforting book.

—ROYREE JENSEN
Senior minister, River of Life Church
Brisbane, Australia

Katherine's authentic ministry is an inspiration to many who desire to see God's kingdom manifest on the earth. Her desire to know the Father's heart brings a solid understanding of how important it is to walk in the miraculous.

Several years ago I gave Katherine a prophecy that she will walk in the same type of mantle as Kathryn Kuhlman did. I am excited to see that unveil as I read of the miraculous testimonies that God is doing in her life. I believe many who read this book will never be the same again.

—Adam F. Thompson
Co-planter, Field of Dreams Australia

It has been such a pleasure for us to know Katherine Ruonala and now to read her book *Living in the Miraculous*. Both her personal ministry as well as her writings carry such an impartation of the Father's jovial heart toward His children. Very early in the book she tells us that "God is always happy to see us," and she is able to make us feel that this is really true. This is clearly a foundational premise for expecting and experiencing the supernatural dimension. As you read this book, you will find your spirit lifted and challenged to go after this very good God who thoroughly enjoys being "scandalously" kind. We highly endorse Katherine Ruonala and this book and believe it will greatly assist in raising up an army of healers who will go after sickness and disease in individuals—and ultimately in the structures of society itself.

—Johnny and Elizabeth Enlow
Authors, *The Seven Mountain Prophecy*,
The Seven Mountain Mantle, and *Rainbow God*

Katherine Ruonala's journey is truly fascinating! It's more like a dance than a step-by-step approach that can sweep you off your feet into the romance and power of living in the miraculous! Not only does she walk in amazing joy and miraculous power personally, but also she and Tom have become spiritual parents to a revolution in their own city of Brisbane, Australia! Week after week her spiritual sons and daughters go out into the streets and demonstrate the power and the joy of the gospel, emptying hospital beds of the sick and dying, and leading many into a loving and faith-filled relationship with our heavenly Father! This book could change you! It is a life-giving message of faith and love that releases the glory of God.

—DR. CHARLES STOCK
Author, *Glow in the Dark*
Senior leader, Life Center Ministries
Harrisburg, PA

Living in the
Miraculous

Living in the
Miraculous

How GOD's LOVE is
expressed through the
Supernatural

KATHERINE
RUONALA

CHARISMA
HOUSE

Cover design by Bill Johnson

Visit the author's website at www.katherineruonala.com.

Library of Congress Cataloging-in-Publication Data:
Ruonala, Katherine.
  Living in the miraculous / Katherine Ruonala. -- First edition.
       pages cm
  ISBN 978-1-62136-284-5 (trade paper) -- ISBN 978-1-62136-285-2 (e-book)
  1. Christian life. 2. Miracles. 3. Supernatural. 4. Pentecostalism. I. Title.
  BV4509.5.R865 2013
  234'.13--dc23
                                              2013013785

While the author has made every effort to provide accurate telephone numbers and Internet addresses at the time of publication, neither the publisher nor the author assumes any responsibility for errors or for changes that occur after publication.

15 16 17 18 19 — 9 8 7 6 5 4
Printed in the United States of America

This book is dedicated to You, Lord, my heavenly Father and best friend. How great You are! Yours is the kingdom, the power, and the glory.

I would also like to dedicate this book to the following people who have helped me in this journey into the miraculous power of God's love:

My husband, Tom: thank you for your love and patience and for the peace that you bring to our lives. I am so grateful for your wisdom, kindness, and companionship. What a blessing to be married to you!

My children, Jessica, Emily, and Joseph: thank you for the delight you bring to our lives. Thinking about you provokes me to worship God for His goodness. I love you all.

All our Glory City Church family and leaders: for your love, passionate commitment to the kingdom and for cultivating a supernatural culture where miracles are an everyday event.

My interns, "the Justice League": you all inspire and delight my heart. I love you very dearly.

Sheila Williams, my faithful friend: thank you for supporting and encouraging me as we have had adventures around the world.

My father, Jim: you inspire me with your compassionate heart. Thank you for believing in me from the beginning. I love you.

Ron and Judith Fearneyhough: for your passion for revival and for your love.

My mum, Roslyn, for introducing me to Jesus. You have given me the greatest gift of my life, and I will be eternally grateful. I love you.

Contents

Acknowledgments

- To Cindy Jacobs and Mahesh Chavdah for your prophetic provocation to write.

- A huge thank-you to Chris Tiegreen for your wonderful help with the manuscript. I so appreciate your gift and all the help and encouragement you have given. You have helped make this book possible, and I am so grateful for your efforts.

- To my mother, Roslyn Mills, for all your work in the editing process

- To Sheila Williams, Sarah Cheesman, Tony Slaughter, Heather Montgomerie, and Chris Wyman: thank you all for your help with the proofreading process. I am so grateful for your help.

Foreword

As you open the pages of *Living in the Miraculous,* you will find yourself immersed in a life-change. The truths that unfold in these chapters are drawn from an intense and profound testimony of the power that flows from relationship with God.

Katherine Ruonala is being used by God to radically impact a generation of young people who have been broken by life—just as she used to be. She has plumbed the Word of God and discovered the key to living a transformed life.

To share her stories and insights has taken courage. There is always risk involved in such an undertaking. However, the benefit will be clearly felt and will help so many find the power of living a supernatural life. As you read this book and God begins to bring you to new depths of joy, you too will become an overcomer just like Katherine.

My preacher-daddy used to say, "Great people are willing to take big risks; small people rarely do because they are afraid to fail. However, great people do great things for God." Katherine's strength in taking risks of faith will release many! If you see yourself on some level in the following pages, allow the transformational truths Katherine reveals to reach deep inside your heart.

Many people struggle with the question "Does God really love me?" Like most of us Katherine has had to wrestle with this question herself. The answers God gave her allowed her not only to come out on the other side but also to help others experience His healing grace—and to live the kind of miraculous life that will bring God's love and liberty to others.

In this book Katherine chips away at all the familiar excuses and shows us how to truly walk in the miraculous. As a little girl I struggled with the issue of fear. I think that our archenemy the devil particularly wants those who are to be used of God to be bound up by paralyzing fear. Katherine addresses this issue, and the truth of the Word of God shines clear as she trumpets, "Perfect love casts out fear!" Fear is a destiny destroyer. Katherine learned how to not be defeated and will lead you out of its snare.

In her chapter about having "yummy Daddy time" she reminds us of the importance of taking time out to fellowship with God. Many people, including myself, get so busy with the responsibilities of life and ministry, but if we truly want our lives to remain fruitful, we have to stop and soak in God's presence and get our souls refreshed.

This book is good for what ails the soul! One of the most helpful truths to every Christian is the reminder in chapter 8 that God will give you "double for your trouble." None of your hurts and pains, none of the difficulties you've experienced in life are wasted. God is in the restoration business!

I can think of a few things right now over which I am going to proclaim, "I am going to get double for my trouble!" What the enemy tried to use to tear down and destroy, God will use to build us and His kingdom. That chapter alone is worth owning this book and giving it as a gift to all your friends!

Because Katherine has written these victorious truths out of the depths of experience, she writes with great authority. These are not "borrowed truths" from someone else's life; she has lived them.

Through the years I have known many women leaders and watched them emerge into their ministries. Katherine's work with youth and the astounding measure of the miraculous she is experiencing tells me she is one of those, like the generals of old such as Kathryn Kuhlman, who will shake the face of the earth.

Read these pages and drink in their contents. Then prepare to be changed!

—CINDY JACOBS

Cofounder, Generals International

Dallas, Texas

Introduction

W HEN OUR MINISTRY team met Christopher at the Royal Brisbane Hospital, there was gangrene in the joints of his hand and he couldn't move his thumb. The tendons had been severed. He said his hand felt heavy and dead. But after the team prayed for him, he said his hand suddenly felt lighter, and he could move his thumb. God had been preparing him for this supernatural encounter for weeks; he had heard the gospel from some Christians who lived in his building. So when his hand was healed after he received prayer, Christopher was ready to give his life to the Lord.

A young woman in the same hospital that night was experiencing severe pain from pancreatitis. She too felt lighter when we prayed over her, and the pain began to subside. The woman's condition improved so much after that night of prayer, she was released from the hospital several days earlier than expected.

Just a week earlier one of our team leaders, Chris Turner, approached a young man whose body was rejecting a recent cornea transplant. He had no sight in his eye, but as the team started praying for him, he began to see colors and then a light that made him jump. Asked what was happening, the man said a light was getting closer and closer. Then he could see with some definition, and then finally he had perfect vision! He knew Jesus had come and healed him, so he gave his life to Christ. We found out that his mother was a pastor; her prayers for his salvation had been answered that night. The doctors confirmed that he no longer needed a second operation and sent him home the next day.

After praying for people at the hospital, the team went to King George Square in central Brisbane, Australia, to pray for people on the streets. Before going out, team members had sensed God directing them to one specific location, so that's where they went first. When they arrived, they met a man named Robert who, along with his family, had nowhere to stay the night. Robert had been in an accident in 1984 that left him in a coma for a year and a half, and ever since he had awakened in 1985, he had felt pain in his head.

He was depressed and suicidal when our team encountered him. When they asked how they could pray for him, he mentioned only that his children had nowhere to sleep. He wanted them to be safe. But God had much bigger plans for him. Within minutes of receiving prayer, a person Robert had never met, who happened to be from a local homeless agency, walked up to him and offered to book a hotel room for him and his family that night.

Not only that, but the pain in his head also disappeared. His depression turned to joy and amazement. He gave his heart and his life to Jesus because, as he said, "This can't be a coincidence." He had experienced the good heart of the Father answering a prayer and meeting his needs.[1]

Today I received this joyful report from James Markert, one of our ministry school students:

> Dead Man Raised Back to Life!
> I experienced a sovereign move of the Spirit in a pharmacy at Ashgrove yesterday around 3:00 p.m. As I walked toward the front counter

of the store, a large elderly man in his seventies about a meter away from me had a major heart attack. Three staff members put him in a chair, and he started convulsing. Then the staff placed him flat on the floor to administer CPR. When he was placed on the floor, he became clinically dead for about two minutes. His heart stopped beating, his lungs stopped breathing, his eyes stopped blinking and were opened as if he were in a trance, and there was no movement. The elderly man's wife kept saying, "Is he breathing?"

I felt God challenge me by saying, "What are you going to do about it?" I quickly rushed over to the staff and said, "I am a Christian." The CPR did not seem to be working, as the elderly man, as I found out, had a history of heart problems and was actually carrying heart tablets in his pocket. I felt led to prophesy life over him, and as I laid my hand on his leg, my hand went to pins and needles. I felt something like electricity flow through my hand, and soon after, the elderly man started coughing, and signs of life came back into his body—glory to God!

The man doing the CPR told me, "Thank you for praying," as he realized there had been divine intervention in this elderly man's body. The female staff member took down my name and phone number for anyone who wanted to say thank you. God is so awesome![2]

These stories sound like the rare, miraculous experiences that we used to talk about as believers for months after they happened, but these kinds of occurrences are becoming the new "normal." Our ministry teams go into the streets and hospitals and malls of Brisbane every week and into the markets with our "Shekinah tent" on Saturdays and Sundays to pray for people and let God show them His good heart. Through words of knowledge and demonstrations of the Spirit's power many people are coming to Christ. It has come to the point now that we have to ask those who lead people to Christ to be responsible to baptize them; it's the only way we can practically keep up with the numbers. One of our members actually carries a mobile "baptism kit" in his car. It's comprised of board shorts, T-shirts, and towels. People are being delivered of drug addictions and more as they are baptized. We are seeing God's kindness as He miraculously meets the needs of people who desperately need to know Him. This is revival.

I believe what we are seeing in Brisbane is part of a sovereign move of God taking place around the world. This isn't just happening in our church; it's happening in many places on every continent. Recently on a return visit to Augusta, Georgia, for example, I met a man named Bobby Rogers who had come to one of my meetings five years ago, saying he had terminal cancer. Doctors had given him only a few months to live, as the cancer had begun in his colon and had spread to his liver and lungs before they had discovered it. But he saw me on TV and found that I would be ministering at a church in Augusta, not far from his home.

He asked a friend to take him to the meeting. I remember praying for him there and declaring, "This man has faith!" During my recent visit—now several years after that meeting—he told me the rest of the story. He had gone home that night and slept like a baby, and he said the next time he went to the doctor, he told the doctor he had been healed and wasn't going to die. He said the doctor agreed that patients who pray tend to live longer, but it was unlikely the physician had ever seen a patient quite like him. Bobby has gained weight and is feeling great. That's just one example of what's happening everywhere. The supernatural revelation of God's love is radically transforming people, cities, and nations. It's unlocking fearless faith.

Is faith the key to seeing miracles such as these? Many believers long for greater faith because they know that is what moves mountains. If we could "only believe," we would see more miracles. Isn't that what we've always been taught? The Bible tells us that anything is possible for those who believe; God will do great works if we learn to live by faith.

Without knowing the One we put our faith in, our attempts to believe Him are futile.

That's true, of course, but there's a deeper issue than faith. So many people struggle with this dynamic of growing in faith in order to see more miracles. It isn't that we doubt the promises of God; we're more inclined to doubt that we have enough faith to see those promises manifest in our lives. When we don't see miracles and manifestations of the power of God as often as we want to, we begin to question whether our faith is enough—whether it's big enough or pure enough or consistent enough.

I believe the reason for this is that without knowing the One we put our faith in, our attempts to believe Him are futile. Unless the Holy Spirit gives us a revelation of who God is, believing Him will continue to be a struggle. We have to get a vision of His true nature and know how He sees us. Or, more specifically, we have to have a revelation of His love.

Scripture tells us that faith works by love (Gal. 5:6). Experiencing the love of God unleashes the faith God has given us, and it allows us to trust Him with a glorious abandonment. God wants us to become rooted and grounded in His love so we can enter the rest of faith. He wants us to be so confident in His love that we don't even hesitate to boldly approach the throne of grace. When we really get a glimpse of His extravagant, relentless love for us—when we look into His eyes and are overwhelmed by how much He adores us—we stop struggling to have faith. We just have it. We believe because we see who He is.

How can we get this vision of His love? Well, for starters, we can ask for it. Ephesians 3:14–21 is one of my favorite apostolic prayers, and it's all about this very desire we have to know our Father's love.

> For this reason I bow my knees before the Father, from whom every family in heaven and on earth derives its name, that He would grant you, according to the riches of His glory, to be strengthened with power through His Spirit in the inner man, so that Christ may dwell in your hearts through faith; and that you, being rooted and grounded in love, may be able to comprehend with all the saints what is the breadth and length and height and depth, and to know the love of Christ which surpasses knowledge, that you may be filled up to all the fullness of God.
>
> Now to Him who is able to do far more

abundantly beyond all that we ask or think,
according to the power that works within us, to
Him be the glory in the church and in Christ
Jesus to all generations forever and ever. Amen.
—Ephesians 3:14–21, nas

Do you see the heart of this request? Paul prays that
the Holy Spirit would strengthen us in our inner being for
one specific purpose: so we would be able to comprehend
this love that completely surpasses natural understanding.
He prays that we would know the height and the depth and
the width and the breadth of that love, and even that we
would be filled with all the fullness of God, who is love. As
God's love overflows in our lives, we are delivered—from
fear, from distractions, from obstacles, from all the mess
that gets into our lives—and we are released to trust the
One who then wants to do exceedingly abundantly above
all we can ask, hope, or imagine.

This prayer links His love with our experience of His
power. As we will see, this is a key to our ability to have
faith. We have to be able to live out of the knowledge of
God's love in order to know who we are, to know how He
sees us, and to know how to enter into the intimacy He
calls us to experience. When we can fully rest in His love,
faith flourishes and miracles begin to flow.

This relationship between knowing God's love and
seeing His power is part of God's plan to reveal Himself
through those who know Him. We are gateways, and God
wants to step through us. The more we are able to experience His nature, the more we are able to demonstrate
His nature to others. Scripture tells us that all of creation
longs to see the children of God revealed (Rom. 8:19), and

as we draw closer to Him and rest in who He is, He shows Himself through us.

I believe that God manifesting Himself through us is the result of a great awakening that has already begun. I am seeing this awakening all across the body of Christ and throughout the nations. People from all walks of life and denominations are having the eyes of their understanding enlightened in the knowledge of God and as a result are waking up to the hope of their calling, the riches of His glorious inheritance, and the greatness of His power toward those who believe. That's an answer to another great apostolic prayer that Paul prayed:

> I also, after I heard of your faith in the Lord Jesus and your love for all the saints, do not cease to give thanks for you, making mention of you in my prayers: that the God of our Lord Jesus Christ, the Father of glory, may give to you the spirit of wisdom and revelation in the knowledge of Him, the eyes of your understanding being enlightened; that you may know what is the hope of His calling, what are the riches of the glory of His inheritance in the saints, and what is the exceeding greatness of His power toward us who believe, according to the working of His mighty power which He worked in Christ when He raised Him from the dead and seated Him at His right hand in the heavenly places, far above all principality and power and might and dominion, and every name that is named, not only in this age but also in that which is to come.
>
> —EPHESIANS 1:15–21

Yes, the Spirit of wisdom and revelation is waking people up to the truth of who God really is and to the truly free gift of His amazing grace. As a result of this awakening, we are now seeing some of the glorious miracles we used to only dream about. The testimonies I shared at the opening are only a taste of what's to come. We are receiving reports of cancerous tumors disappearing, of incurable diseases being healed, of the deaf hearing, and of glorious, instant creative miracles. Recently a doctor referred one of his patients to our church because he had heard about people receiving deliverance from addictions. That same night the patient was saved, healed, and delivered.

We are now entering the greatest harvest
of souls the world has ever seen.

Once people experience a touch from God, they are transformed and immediately want to share their transformation with their family and friends. It's so beautiful to see new believers who have been birthed in a supernatural culture so easily step out in their God-given gifts as the Holy Spirit breathes new life into their spirits.

People all over the world are being provoked to worship God with a fresh awe as they see His power at work. The harvest is so ripe! We are now entering the greatest harvest of souls the world has ever seen. A fresh awakening has begun, and the eyes of our understanding are being enlightened in the knowledge of how good God really is. The apostolic prayers are still being answered in amazing ways in our generation.

It is a glorious time to be alive. God has laid up so many good works in advance for you to do, and He wants to gloriously exceed your wildest dreams. He wants to use you and me in the harvest. He doesn't expect us to win the world with persuasive words of human wisdom but with demonstrations of His power. These demonstrations will come through those who have encountered the love of God that passes knowledge. Those who know the One who is love will be strong and do great exploits (Dan. 11:32)! My prayer as you read this book is that the Holy Spirit will awaken your heart to His unrelenting love and set you free to believe.

Chapter 1

UNDERSTANDING THE FATHER'S HEART

Unfair Kindness and Scandalous Grace

A S THE HOLY Spirit is awakening His church to prepare for the harvest of souls, He is releasing revelation in ways that are both glorious and life changing, and it is empowering people to do the works of Jesus. This revelation is healing people body, soul, and spirit. We're shifting from human thinking to kingdom understanding, from powerless Christianity to remarkable signs and miracles, from working for God to resting in Him and letting Him work through us. But all of these wonderful changes have been prefaced with an outpouring of something much more foundational: the revelation of the Father's heart.

> We need to have a mind-renewing revelation of His love.

I believe the apostolic prayer in Ephesians 3 gives us a prophetic road map of the final great awakening that is beginning to manifest in the world. We looked at this passage in the introduction, but let's read it again and focus specifically on what it says about God's love:

> I bow my knees before the Father, from whom every family in heaven and on earth derives its name, that He would grant you, according to the riches of His glory, to be strengthened with power through His Spirit in the inner man, so that Christ may dwell in your hearts through faith; *and that you, being rooted and grounded in love, may be able to comprehend with all the saints what is the breadth and length and height and depth, and to know the love of Christ which surpasses knowledge,* that you may be filled up to all the fullness of God.
> —EPHESIANS 3:14–19, NAS,
> emphasis added

Paul follows this prayer with some words of praise for the One who is able to do "exceedingly abundantly above all" that we can ask or even think (v. 20). But I don't think we can really open our hearts to receive the blessings that are exceedingly abundantly above our comprehension unless we really understand who God is. Most Christians don't feel deep in their hearts that God is *for* us—that He's always happy to see us and is overflowing with love for us. But He is!

We may feel like the bride in the Song of Solomon felt—dark, dry, unlovely, unworthy, never measuring up—but the King looks at us and says, "You're so lovely!" That's all He can see in us. He looks through the sacrifice of His Son's life and sees purity and beauty in us. He qualifies us to enter His throne room, the holy place of His presence, at any time. He calls us the apple of His eye. If our hearts don't grasp this amazing truth, we can't open ourselves up enough to experience all that He wants to do for us and with us. We need to have a mind-renewing revelation of His love.

FAITH WORKS BY LOVE

It's interesting that immediately after Paul's prayer for us to know the love of Christ that passes knowledge, he goes on to proclaim:

> Now to Him who is able to do far more abundantly beyond all that we ask or think, according to the power that works within us, to Him be the glory in the church and in Christ Jesus to all generations forever and ever. Amen.
> —EPHESIANS 3:20–21, NAS

The result of continuously exploring the unending, bottomless revelation of the Father's love through the Holy Spirit is that we will be overflowing with all the fullness of God. That overflowing fullness will unlock faith in us that will see Him glorified in ways more wonderful than we have ever imagined. Faith works by love, and miracles will spring forth immeasurably from a life unlocked by this love. That's why I've said that Ephesians 3:14–21 is a prophetic road map for our times. Notice the progression: as the release of the revelation of the Father's love for us comes, so will the filling-to-overflowing and the miracles, signs, and wonders that are exceedingly, abundantly above anything we have dreamed of.

I have begun to see the fruit of abiding in this love, and it never ceases to amaze me. One of the first and most amazing miracles I saw God do through me was for a Baptist woman who came forward for prayer at a meeting in Australia. After explaining that she was Baptist and did not speak in tongues or fall down under God's power, she politely asked if I would pray for her. I was quite excited because the day before, an evangelist named Ian McCormack had prophesied that I would see tumors disappear. The woman had a tumor, and I had a word! So I laid hands on her and prayed. She fell to the ground under the power of God.

I didn't know it at the time, but this woman had undergone an operation to remove a large cancerous tumor in her abdomen. Despite the surgery, the woman said the doctors had not been able to remove the cancer. They were going to try radiation treatment but were not optimistic about her prognosis. That was the condition she was in when she came to the meeting.

After receiving prayer, the woman went back to her doctors, and she said they couldn't find the tumor or any case of cancer. She shared her story at a local women's ministry, and the excitement among the ladies was glorious. The woman's husband then gave his life to Christ and testified to his gratitude and amazement regarding her healing.

Paul prays in Ephesians that we would be able to comprehend the breadth and length and height and depth of God's unquenchable love. Then God can do the works that are "exceedingly abundantly" beyond our imagination, those things He wants to do through the power that works within us—His power that we can experience while we're resting and trusting in Him. This revelation of love is the basis of the awakening that is coming to our generation. And it begins by knowing who God really is.

So Who Is God?

Jesus gave us a powerful picture of what His Father is like when He told the parable of the prodigal son (Luke 15:11–32). It's the story of a rebellious, wayward boy who demanded his inheritance from his father and then set off to live life his way. He squandered everything before being forced by circumstances to consider returning home. Because of his past behavior, he assumed his father would no longer welcome him as a son, but he hoped that possibly his father might have mercy on him and give him work as a servant.

He was living with a sense of condemnation. His thoughts were based on an understanding of love that is natural and human. Human experience teaches us that when we hurt someone, they usually take offense and close off part of their hearts to us. Generally the only way to get them to open their hearts to us again is by demonstrating true remorse and then proving over time that we are trustworthy. This son assumed that because of his behavior, he had burned his bridges with his father and could now only hope, at best, for a position as a servant.

One of the greatest revelations I have ever received is that God's love for me is not based on my behavior. Even while we were still sinners, God loved us and gave Himself for us (Rom. 5:8). The love of God doesn't change toward us. Whether we are good, bad, or ugly, He loves each of us entirely. When we mess up, we aren't surprising Him.

5

He knew what we were going to do ahead of time and still chose to place His affection on us. As author Graham Cooke says, God is never disillusioned with us because He never had any illusions about us to begin with! He is never annoyed with us to the point that He will stop loving us. Even if we don't love Him back, He still loves us powerfully and intensely.

There was a time when I struggled to believe that truth. I knew in theory that God loved me—after all, didn't the Bible tell me so? My mind accepted this as a fact. But in my heart I felt as if God just tolerated me because He had to. Whenever I sinned, I felt I had to work hard to regain even that place of tolerated acceptance again. Like the prodigal son, my understanding of love was natural and human.

I remember praying and confessing my sins one day as I was driving in the car. It was my usual practice to go over anything and everything I'd ever done or could think of and ask forgiveness for it, just in case I hadn't repented properly the previous time I had asked. But as I asked God that particular day to once again forgive me for everything I might have done wrong, I felt Him interrupt me. I had just been pleading, "God, forgive me for this and that, and for all the sins I've ever committed," when He spoke to me and said, "OK." That was all. Just "OK," as if it were all settled.

I didn't know what to do with that response! It was such a shock to me. Suddenly I realized I spent 90 percent of my prayer life repenting of things for which I'd already asked forgiveness. Ephesians 2:8–9 tells us that we are saved by grace through faith in Christ and not of works, which means our forgiveness is based entirely on

His love for us. He had already forgiven me, and I was just persisting in unbelief.

The truth of the gospel is that Jesus saw what I would do before I even did it and paid the penalty for it in advance. What was lacking on my part was faith, not only in His forgiveness but also in His character. So many times I have felt a need to repent "properly"—that a quick sorry wouldn't be enough. This is how it works with human beings we've offended, so that's how we think it works with God. Guilt should lead us to reach out and receive mercy, but often I felt as though I needed to really grieve for a time and let my sins weigh heavily on me until I had emotionally "paid" for them. I thought that the answer to redemption was to spend time dwelling in the dark places of my soul. Human nature likes the idea of doing something for ourselves, of feeling that we've worked hard enough to earn God's mercy. But that's really a form of self-righteousness.

Think of how Jesus forgave Peter for denying Him three times. Peter had cursed and sworn he didn't know Jesus. That's a pretty offensive sin, and Peter felt terrible about it. Judas betrayed Jesus and didn't know how to deal with his regret; he ended up killing himself, as though he were trying to pay for what he had done. But when Peter came to Jesus after His resurrection, the Lord helped him see that His love not only offered forgiveness but also qualification for ministry. And as if it was a sign of God's redemption, we see that on the Day of Pentecost Peter is used as the chief spokesperson to speak to the crowds.

God has already forgiven us, and all we have to do is receive it by faith. He doesn't want us to live under a sense of condemnation. Romans 8:1 says, "There is therefore now no condemnation to those who are in Christ

Jesus." The word *in* (*en* in Greek) used in this passage can be translated "positioned at rest."[1] He essentially says, "There is no condemnation for those who are resting in faith in Me, as part of My body." We are part of Him when we receive His life, part of His body, and He won't condemn Himself. John expresses it another way: "There is no fear in love; instead, perfect love drives out fear, because fear involves punishment. So the one who fears has not reached perfection in love. We love because He first loved us" (1 John 4:18–19, HCSB). That doesn't fit our human understanding, but this is God's way whether we understand it or not.

God's love cannot be interpreted through the filter of our human experience, and as the beautiful parable of the prodigal son reveals, His love is not like the human love we experience on a daily basis. His love is so surprisingly kind! It is a love that passes all of our understanding.

When we receive His mercy by faith, we
are qualified in every way.

This is the kind of love the prodigal son didn't yet know as he journeyed back home. When the father saw his wayward son walking in the distance, he didn't put a look of displeasure on his face. Instead he ran toward him, wrapped his arms around him, and kissed him. Then the son was even more amazed when the father ordered his servants to bring a ring and a robe. He put the ring, representing his own authority, on his son's finger, and he put the robe (like the robe of righteousness that God puts on us) around his shoulders. He then threw a party to celebrate the return of his child! The father could not contain the delight of his heart now that his son had come home.

Do you understand what this says about God's love? It says that regardless of how you have behaved, God's love for you remains the same. While many believers walk around with a guilty conscience and feel disqualified to receive God's promises, we are able to enter a level of freedom that assures us we are qualified at any moment to boldly enter His presence, to shine with His glory, and to do great exploits for His kingdom. We are righteous not because of what we do but because He has made us righteous. The prodigal son was accepted not because he groveled or earned the father's favor. He was accepted simply because he came home to a father who loved him unconditionally.

God accepts us just as freely and with the same enthusiasm and love. If the enemy can make us feel disqualified because we haven't lived perfectly, he can keep us from believing we are qualified to receive the promises of God. We become afraid to lay hands on the sick or behave as heirs of the promises until we can measure up, which, of course, can never happen through our own efforts. But our qualifications are not based on *our* works; they are based on *His*! When we receive His mercy by faith, we are qualified in every way. It is no longer we who live but Christ who lives in us, and He is perfect! God has already clothed us in His robe of righteousness and given us His ring of authority. And we are always welcome to fellowship with Him intimately and receive all that He wants to give us.

ALWAYS HAPPY TO SEE US

This is the revelation that has changed my life. God is *always* happy to see us. Always. God has given us a position seated with Christ in heavenly places. We are coheirs with Him as soon as we believe. We are *in* Him—fully at rest and fully identified with Him. He has made it clear that He doesn't want us to remain at a distance, and He has taken away everything that would hinder us from coming closer. He wants us right there with Him, as close as we can get, in deep, intimate fellowship. While we may feel too unworthy or too unlovely, He sees us as His beloved people who are so valuable to Him. He paid a very high price for us to come close, and He calls us beautiful.

> You have the power to fill a longing in
> God's heart that no one else can fill.

If it has been a while since you've talked to God, then you need to realize He has cleared the path for you to approach Him. He isn't waiting to tell you off or annihilate you with a bolt of lightning, nor has He closed off part of His heart to you. God is not standing at a distance, accusing you of being a hypocrite by trying to come to Him after all you have done. No! Every time you lift your hands to worship Him or cry out to Him in prayer, He runs toward you with love in His eyes and joy in His heart.

In fact, He created you to minister to Him. You have the power to fill a longing in God's heart that no one else can fill. He has torn the veil that separated you from Him,

10

and He invites you into His presence to be embraced by Him, to bless Him, and to be blessed by Him. "Let us then approach the throne of grace with confidence, so that we may receive mercy and find grace to help us in our time of need" (Heb. 4:16, NIV). That's your purpose!

It's a stunning thought, isn't it? You bless God. His heart beats faster by your desire to know Him better and to be with Him. So all of these perceptions we have about Him, like being reluctant to welcome us because we haven't measured up, are simply false. Nothing, not even your worst sin, can keep you at a distance if you're willing to come. God always wants you to come closer because He loves you.

Morning and evening God stands ready to restore your soul and bring you beauty for ashes. He wants you to know this and to have a growing awareness of His celebration over you. He cannot contain the delight in His heart when you use your free will to choose to come to Him. He never says, "That's a good try, but your voice isn't as good as my other children's voices. I've heard better music than that. And I wish you had more enthusiasm."

You may feel pathetic in your efforts to worship Him or to have a good prayer time, but He feels very differently. He rejoices in the fact that He captured your heart, even if just for that moment. Whenever you come to Him, the very moment you take a step in His direction, even if you think you're coming with a feeble attempt to worship, He bends low to listen to you. He rejoices over you with singing (Zeph. 3:17). When my children come to me for a cuddle, my heart lights up with joy. In the same way, when we come with our hands up like little children asking to be picked up and cuddled, God can't resist! Your love delights your Father's heart.

SCANDALOUS GRACE

When the prodigal son's older brother heard of how the father had lavished his love on such an unworthy rebel— how his younger brother was instantly restored with full authority and blessing—he didn't respond very well. He misunderstood the father's heart. Even though he was a son with all the family privileges, the older brother worked with a servant mentality. Though he could have been living with joy all along and receiving the father's bless- ings without having to earn them, he had instead based his status on his behavior.

He had spent a lot of time and effort trying to be the good son. Because he felt as though he had behaved so much better than his younger brother, he was outraged by the joy his father felt at his younger brother's return. When the father tried to encourage him to join the party and rejoice, the older brother responded with judgment and anger.

Sadly the message of grace can be offensive to those who have lived their lives under the dictates of man-made religious rules. The religious spirit tries to convince us that works are the key to receiving kingdom benefits. It compels us to compare ourselves with others, leading us either to judgment of others or to self-condemnation. This is what Scripture calls the way of the flesh (Rom. 8), and it's never enough. The requirements are never satisfied. It's as if someone is dangling a carrot in front of you that you will never be able to catch.

Martin Luther tried to live this way, determined to kill the flesh and be holy, and he almost died in the process. That's how he came to a fresh revelation that the just live by faith and are saved by God's grace alone. He learned that religious spirits try to lead us on a never-ending chase for righteousness, and it's futile. But this scandalous grace of God is offensive to those who are still in the middle of the chase. Often unknowingly they are trusting in their flesh to become righteous and be accepted, and when someone completely unworthy—like the prodigal son— is fully accepted without having earned that right, they become indignant.

We can live according to the lies of this religious spirit in very subtle ways. When I first started preaching, I was in the habit of fasting the day I was due to minister, assuming that my fasting would increase the anointing I would operate under. The problem came when I was asked to preach every day. I couldn't physically fast every day, so I was faced with the dilemma of having to decide which meetings I could afford to be less anointed for. I didn't realize until years later that my reasoning was all wrong. If my fasting increased the measure of anointing available to me, then it would also mean that I could take some of the glory for the anointing I had "earned" by my self-sacrifice. I'm not saying that fasting is wrong. In fact, I believe in having a lifestyle of prayer and fasting. A God-ordained fast is completely different and can be powerful for increasing and feeding our spiritual appetites—but my heart wasn't in the right place when I was fasting in order to get the anointing. What I had been doing was flowing from a legalistic, old-wineskin mentality.

This works-based mind-set usually comes with a lot

of accusation and guilt. Satan comes to us and whispers subtle accusations. "All those poor people in India, and look at you—having dessert. Isn't that just a bit selfish?" Or he'll suggest, "You think you're pleasing to God having prayed for an hour today? Didn't you notice how your mind wandered? It wasn't really an hour, now, was it? And why weren't you trying for two hours anyway? You filled the rest of your day with far less worthy pursuits, didn't you?"

This is what brings Him joy.
Faith pleases God.

This voice can condemn us over almost anything, and it often doesn't take much for us to believe it. The reason we so easily believe the lies of the enemy is that he disguises himself to look and sound like us. The enemy will try to deceive you into believing the condemning lies by making you think your own heart is condemning you. But no matter how hard you try to appease this voice, you never will. You'll never arrive at holiness by trying to follow a set of religious rules.

I'm so thankful God has made another way for us. He delights to give us the kingdom and all His authority, not because of what we do but because we have humbled ourselves to receive His unmerited favor. It's His pleasure to lavish on us the blessings of His goodness. He did all the work to make it possible; we rest in Him and receive it. This is what brings Him joy. Faith pleases God.

Understanding this truth about God's heart means you never again have to labor under the condemning voice of a religious spirit. Now when you feel compassion for somebody in the shopping center, you can know you are instantly and always qualified to release the power of Jesus because God has qualified you. He has taken care of everything that stands between you and Him, everything that would hinder your anointing. Instead of listening to the voice that wants to tell you how much prayer and fasting you haven't done and the reasons you aren't in a good spiritual state, you can be bold and release healing anyway.

The power of God works within you not because of what you have or haven't done but because of what God has done and because of your relationship with Him. Our effort does not bring us to a place of fruitfulness. Simply believing in His power flowing with love through us causes miracles to happen in our lives.

I remember once praying for someone for healing and struggling because I felt no release of power. It seemed the anointing was just bouncing back on me, even though I was doing everything I could think of to see this person healed. Then I felt the Holy Spirit tap me on the shoulder and whisper, "Lean back into Me, and let Me flow through you." As soon as I did, I felt the release of power, and the person was healed. We are gateways of the kingdom, and God wants to step through us, so we just need to rest in Him and let Him!

BEFORE WE EVEN ASK

We see many examples in the Gospels of people who simply received what Jesus offered without having to qualify for it. Perhaps you remember the story of the woman accused of adultery. The religious leaders had caught her in a sinful act, brought her to Jesus, and threw her at His feet. The Law demanded that adulterers must be stoned to death, and the religious leaders could hardly contain their delight. They thought they had trapped this troublemaker Jesus, this friend of sinners. They tried to put Him between two unappealing choices: either deny the Law and forgive her, or deny the mercy He had been preaching and have her stoned.

> But Jesus stooped down and with His finger wrote on the ground. But when they persisted in asking Him, He straightened up, and said to them, "He who is without sin among you, let him be the first to throw a stone at her." Again He stooped down and wrote on the ground. When they heard it, they began to go out one by one, beginning with the older ones, and He was left alone, and the woman, where she was, in the center of the court. Straightening up, Jesus said to her, "Woman, where are they? Did no one condemn you?" She said, "No one, Lord." And Jesus said, "I do not condemn you, either. Go. From now on sin no more."
> —JOHN 8:6–11, NAS

The thing that most amazes me about this event is the fact that this woman did not ask for forgiveness before Jesus said, "Neither do I condemn you." She hadn't said a word. There were no cries for mercy or tearful confessions. Jesus gave her the gift of forgiveness without her even speaking at all. And He didn't even rebuke her. He never said, "I'll forgive you, but just this once," or "I'll show you mercy, but only on the condition that you never do this again," or "If you ask nicely, I'll let you go this time." He simply said He didn't condemn her. He was the only one in the crowd who was without sin and had a right to throw the first stone— He really could have responded to His own challenge—but He chose not to. By giving her the gift of forgiveness, He was empowering her to go and sin no more.

This was mind-boggling for me when I first saw it. How could we be offered forgiveness without first repenting? When John saw Jesus coming to be baptized, he declared, "Behold! The Lamb of God who takes away the sin of the world!" (John 1:29). Jesus paid for our sins before we were ever born—all of them, even the ones we haven't committed yet—and He now stands offering forgiveness to the whole world. He looked ahead to all we would do, all the mistakes we would make, all the sins we would commit, and chose us anyway.

He doesn't look at us thinking, "Hmm, I'm not sure yet whether I'll let this one into the kingdom." He doesn't suddenly notice our sin and say, "Oh, I never saw that coming. That changes everything!" No, He offers us "no condemnation" when we believe in Him and rest in what He has done for us. This undeserved kindness is offered to you in the hope that you will respond by humbling yourself and receiving that which you can have no part in earning.

This woman wasn't the only one in the Gospels who was offered undeserved grace before she asked for it. Jesus did a similar thing for a lame man who was let down through the roof by his friends. He simply looked at him and said, "Your sins are forgiven you" (Mark 2:5). The lame man had not even spoken. There it is again—scandalous grace! Jesus Christ, who the Bible says was slain from the foundation of the world, can forgive us before we even ask for it! I'm not saying that we don't need to ask for forgiveness, of course. What I'm saying is that we often think God's grace is based on how well we show Him we deserve it. We often think we're repenting when we're actually beating ourselves up in an attitude of penance, with little or no faith in His grace, believing instead that our degree of self-deprecation is what accomplishes our forgiveness.

But this is just another human effort in disguise. God's grace comes to us freely. The Bible says that it is "by grace [we] have been saved through faith...not of works, lest anyone should boast" (Eph. 2:8–9). By taking our place on the cross, Jesus Christ paid the price for our sins—past, present, and future. He now stands as the only one who is qualified to offer us forgiveness. In fact, the Bible says He has been slain for the sins of the world. That means He stands ready to offer the gift of forgiveness to anyone who will dare to believe and receive this scandalous grace.

God extends grace to us by forgiving us unconditionally and giving us a new nature through which He empowers us to live righteously. It's the goodness and kindness of God that leads us to repentance (Rom. 2:4). When we see His goodness, our hearts are drawn to Him. Jesus who was crucified before the foundation of the world—He lives outside of time, so His death was a settled matter before our time began—was able to tell the woman caught in adultery to "go and sin no more" because He knew if she believed in Him, she would receive mercy and forgiveness; and if she received that, she would receive the power not to sin. When we receive God's grace, His Spirit reveals to us that we are new creations in Christ and therefore are no longer slaves to sin. The Law enslaves us, but grace sets us free. I'll share more on this in chapter 3.

UNFAIRLY KIND

The good news of the gospel is "unfair" by human standards. God freely offers forgiveness and full restoration to people who have not sought it or even asked for it. Though we aren't naturally qualified to receive anything He offers us, He qualifies us anyway. He simply seeks to provoke us with His kindness in the hope that we will respond by opening our hearts and humbly receiving His undeserved mercy. Jesus, slain from the foundation of the earth, was punished for our sins before you and I were born, so even those sins we have not yet committed have been forgiven. That's how thorough His love for us is.

It takes humility to receive what you know you can have no part in earning and faith to embrace such radical grace. Imagine how wonderful it would be to hear this message of forgiveness, instead of a message of judgment, proclaimed from street corners. That is what is happening on the streets of Brisbane, and the response is glorious. The message of the kindness of God bears far more fruit in people's lives than the condemnation they often hear from Christians. Jesus was known as the friend of sinners. He didn't come into the world to condemn us but to save us. Why? Because He loves us more extravagantly than we can even begin to imagine. And when we really get a revelation of that love, everything changes.

Chapter 2

BEING TRANSFORMED
BY HIS LOVE

Royal Robes and Fearless Love

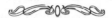

I WAS TWELVE WHEN I was converted after having an incredible encounter with God. It was at a youth camp with Australian healing minister Clark Taylor in 1982 held at Mount Tuchekoi in Queensland. Hundreds of young people were raising their hands and worshipping God, but standing among them, I really struggled with the worship. How do you worship a God you don't know? I wanted to experience Him in a real way. As the worship continued, my heart cried out in a desperate prayer. "God, I believe in You, but I can't see You, and I don't know You, and it's really hard to worship someone I can't see and don't know. Help me!" I knew I needed a heart connection with God and didn't know how else to express my desperation. My best and most honest prayer was, "Help!"

Right in the middle of worship I encountered God in a way that changed my life forever. I saw a vision of the Lord in heaven. Suddenly I could see! My spiritual eyes were opened. God was real! It's difficult for me to describe, but as John Newton penned so beautifully, I could now say,

"Amazing grace, how sweet the sound that saved a wretch like me. I once was lost, but now I'm found, was blind, but now I see."[1]

My mother tells me I was a different person from that time on. I knew I was different too. How could I not be? I had met God personally! My thinking changed, and my desires changed. It was just as 2 Corinthians 5:17 says: those who are in Christ are a new creation. I was different from that day on, forever changed. I went on to be baptized with water and receive the gift of tongues when I was thirteen, and I grew more and more zealous for God. I attended every church meeting I could. If there was an early-morning prayer meeting, I would harass whomever I could find to give me a ride to church. God became my life, and I wanted everything to do with Him.

How do you worship a God you don't know?

Yet despite this wonderful new relationship with God, I struggled with understanding His love. Soon after my conversion my living circumstances changed, and I went through a very difficult time. It's unnecessary to go into detail about this, but I experienced ongoing abuse from someone in my circle of acquaintances. This left me deeply insecure as I struggled with shame, fear, and rejection. The enemy was working hard to destroy the new life that God had given me.

Things like abuse and abandonment can have a deep emotional impact on children that manifests in different ways. Shame, fear, and codependency can all be symptoms that surface because of deeper issues of rejection. I remember coming home from school one day during that time, and our cat had been run over and killed. The lady I was staying with had put some chocolate on my bed and came in to break the bad news as gently as she could. She was a nice person, and it was a very kind thing to do, but I remember distinctly feeling angry inside as she watched me to see my reaction, to see if I would cry.

I suppose I felt like it was all so wrong to have a stranger instead of my mother or father taking care of me. And from that day for the next seven or so years, I found I wasn't able to cry. It was as though I put up a wall that day that even I couldn't get around. When I was older, I would sometimes wish I could cry at times when it seemed appropriate, but still the tears wouldn't come.

I chuckle now when I think of how I have laughed and cried uninhibitedly in front of big crowds. God is so good in the way He heals our hearts and makes us whole. New scientific studies tell us that emotional tears are actually healthy, ridding toxins built up in our body from stress.[2] I like the way the Bible talks about our tears:

> Lord, You know all my desires and deepest
>   longings
> My tears are liquid words
> And You can read them all.
> —PSALM 38:9, TPT

God interprets our tears as words and understands us better than we understand ourselves.

During my school and university years, I managed to keep things together most of the time, serving as a Sunday school teacher and youth leader, but during my early twenties, I was forced to confront what had happened to me when I was a younger teenager. Some people close to me guessed the pain I was trying to hide and wanted to help out, but this was the last thing I wanted. I had hoped it would all just go away if I didn't think about it. But the memories haunted me.

Emotionally and physically I didn't cope as I struggled to shut out painful memories. My body began to misbehave. I was taken in for exploratory surgery, where they found I had mild endometriosis, but the doctors attributed my physical issues to stress.

I was working as a high school music and drama teacher at the time and would often find myself emotionally unable to cope, so I asked the Lord to help me by giving me a part-time job instead. So many people believe that by running away or changing their circumstances, they can escape their inner pain. But sadly, without healing, a change provides only a momentary distraction. I was looking for that kind of distraction. A part-time position at a Christian school became available, and I accepted.

During the orientation week at this school staff members were given an assignment to take a piece of paper and go away for fifteen minutes and write down what the Lord was saying. This was new to me, but I took my piece of paper and went to talk with God. I used to think that every time I went to God, He would have something He wanted to correct in my life—that His main goal was to sort me out. So I was expecting the Lord to give me a list of things I needed to improve.

As I listened, I heard Him say to my heart, "I love you." I wasn't very impressed. I thought, "God, everyone knows

You love them. Can we get on with the program? What do You really want to say? What do I need to fix? Tell me something profound." But over the next fifteen minutes all I could hear Him saying to my heart was, "I love you."

Sometimes on rare occasions God will speak with an audible voice, but most of the time I find He speaks to us with a still, small voice in our spirit. Again and again that's what I heard, and I had to go back to the staff orientation with nothing but those three words. I knew everyone would be sharing what they heard, and I felt like my three words were inadequate—way too simple and obvious, something everyone already knew.

I didn't realize it, but they were the three words I needed to hear the most. I didn't believe I was lovable and felt as though God loved me only because He had to. After all, God loves everyone. In my heart I felt like God must just tolerate me. As a result, my mentality had been that God was always wanting to give instructions and sort us out. Like the Shulamite in the Song of Solomon, we complain, "I know I am so unworthy—so in need!" I thought for sure I was always disappointing God and never quite measuring up.

[The Shulamite]
"Jerusalem maidens,
I know I am so unworthy—so in need!

[The Shepherd-King]
Yet you are so lovely!

[The Shulamite]
I feel as dark and dry as the desert tents
Of the wandering nomads!

25

[The Shepherd-King]
Yet you are so lovely—
Like the fine linen curtains
Of the Holy Place!
—SONG OF SOLOMON 1:5, TPT

When we complain about our unworthiness, God tells us we are lovely. In fact, instead of seeing us as we so often see ourselves—dry and dirty like the desert tents—He compares us to the fine linen curtains of the holy place. Everything in the temple is utterly holy, and this is how He sees us, His bride, sanctified by the blood of the spotless Lamb, Jesus.

He looks at us and says, "But you're so lovely. I love you." And I learned that this *is* His highest priority for us—to enjoy a love relationship with us. And it begins with us receiving His love by faith.[3]

Am I saying God doesn't want us to turn away from sin? Of course not. He has given us power to be holy. But He wants us to believe who He is so we can come close enough to really have our hearts opened to His love. Then when He does need to show us something that's holding us back, we don't run away and hide in shame, because we're already secure in His love. We say, "Oh, Lord, You're right! Thank You for showing me. I receive Your healing and Your forgiveness for that."

The Book of James says that if we are not doers of the Word, it is because we have forgotten what we look like!

If anyone is a hearer of the word and not a doer,
he is like a man who looks at his natural face in
a mirror; for once he has looked at himself and

gone away, he has immediately forgotten what
kind of person he was.

—JAMES 1:23–24, NAS

God wants to remind you that you now look like Him!
And being daily reminded of who we are causes us to live
out of that revelation instead of being deceived. Peter also
talks about the consequences of forgetting what we look
like. In reference to the virtues of God being manifested
through our lives, he writes: "He who lacks these qualities
is blind or short-sighted, having forgotten his purification
from his former sins" (2 Pet. 1:9, NAS).

The Spirit of God is awakening our hearts in the knowledge of Him, calling us to seek His face so we can be continually reminded of what He is like and that we are made
in His image as new creations in Christ.

**He delights in bringing
a smile to our face.**

God wants to make His face shine on us so we trust
Him enough to heal our hearts. If you're like I was, always
looking for what God wants to correct in you, please
understand that He has a higher priority for you. He isn't
waiting for you to come closer so He can smack you or sort
you out. He's urging you to come close because He loves
you and wants you to see the fullness of emotion that's in
His face. He makes His face shine on us and is gracious to
us (Num. 6:25).

Have you ever seen a parent making faces at a baby?

The parent smiles and says goo-goo-gaga in the hope of getting the child to respond with a smile or a laugh. And the joy parents get from seeing that sought-after smile delights their heart. God is a loving parent who makes His face shine on us because He delights in bringing a smile to our face. He provokes us until we respond in joy and worship. We love because He first loved us. When I heard Him say "I love you" that day, I was only beginning to understand that His highest priority was to love us and provoke us to love. Soon I would have an encounter that would change my life.

PERFECT LOVE CASTS OUT FEAR

About a year later, when I was a young mother with a small baby, a visiting speaker who was moving in the gift of healing came to town. In the Sunday morning service he encouraged people who had a need for healing to fast and pray and come back that night. I had a little ganglion cyst on my wrist at the time that was bothering me, and although it was benign, it was painful. As the time came for the night meeting, my husband, Tom, encouraged me to go to the service and offered to watch the baby. Remembering that the minister had asked people to fast and pray, I decided to skip dinner and read Scripture. (I had been eating cakes and all sorts of goodies that day, so I hoped that missing dinner would do!)

I'd recently read a book about having a relationship with the Holy Spirit, so figuring that the Holy Spirit was my Teacher, I decided to ask Him some questions. I asked three things in my car on the way to the meeting that night. First, I remember asking Him to teach me about the whole "falling down under the power of God" thing. I had grown up in a Pentecostal church but was still unsure as to whether people were really being hit by the power of God or if they were being pushed or were just being polite! I wanted to know the truth, so I thought it best to ask the One who is the Spirit of Truth. Second, I asked the Lord to heal my wrist and take away the ganglion cyst. Finally, I asked Him to set me free from a deep, nagging fear I held—the fear that my husband would die.

As someone who had experienced rejection and abandonment as a child, marrying a man who had agreed to love me for the rest of his life was a dream come true. I had met Tom at our youth group and started going out with him when I was eighteen. He really was my knight in shining armor, and we married as soon as I finished university when I was twenty and he was twenty-four. Finally I had someone who made me feel loved! After we were married, I latched onto Tom with an emotional vice-like grip, having heard him vow on our wedding day to love me as long as he lived. Then the thought came—but what if he dies? This fear set in and began to haunt me.

That night the preacher spoke on the scripture I had read instead of eating dinner, which was a great encouragement. Then he invited anyone who had fasted and prayed for a healing to come forward. Not having fasted and prayed for the whole day, I didn't think I really qualified, but I slipped in toward the end of the line anyway.

The evangelist had started praying for people at the other end of what was a long line. As I waited, I lifted my hands, and instantly the power of God buckled my knees, and I hit the floor. As I lay on the ground, I trembled under the power of God. When the minister finally got to me, he asked the ushers to pick me up, he prayed without touching me, and...*whoosh*, I hit the ground again. I received the answer to one of the questions I had asked the Holy Spirit.

As I lay there, I saw the Lord's face. It was overwhelming. He spoke to me gently and with reassuring authority as He said, "Katherine, I am setting you free from everything." The perfect love of God rushed in and set me free from my fears. It felt like I was on the floor for about an hour, and when I was finally able to get up, I felt like I was floating on air. I noticed a few days later that the ganglion cyst on my wrist was gone—that had been my second question. After that encounter my prayer times began to flourish, as I felt free to fellowship with God in a fresh way. The prophetic gift was activated in my life, and I began to see visions and hear the voice of God with a clarity and freedom that I had never experienced before. So that was the beginning of the answer to my third request.

⁓⌇⁓

**One encounter with Him can undo the wounds
that have been plaguing us for years**

The following week there was an altar call for those who had a problem with shame in their lives. I went to the altar again, and after a few people had come past and prayed for me, I heard the Lord ask me to stay. The service was over and the lights started going out. I remained standing and worshipping at the altar, when suddenly the Lord took me into a vision. At first I saw myself as a little child with a really ugly face, and then as I watched, that face just floated away like a mask. Then I saw the Lord with my head on His lap, and He was gently stroking my hair. I'd never had anyone do that for me, and I was so touched by His affection for me.

Then as I kept looking, I saw a woman walking in heaven dressed as royalty in beautiful, flowing robes. The only way I could really describe her was that she was clothed in dignity. As I watched her walk in the heavens with beauty and confidence, the Lord whispered in my ear, "That's you." At the sound of His voice I fell to the floor, laughing and crying. God did in that short time what no psychiatrist could ever have done. In one encounter He restored the dignity I had lost and introduced me to who I really was to Him.

REVELATIONS OF LOVE

This is what God delights to do for each of His children. He comes to us tenderly and affectionately to show us who we really are and how deeply He loves us. When we've experienced rejection and felt the pain of loneliness, as many of us have, we don't naturally grasp His love. But one encounter with Him can undo the wounds that have been plaguing us for years and distorting our view of His heart.

God doesn't just limit His revelation to one encounter, however. He reveals Himself to us again and again if we seek Him and trust that He wants to show Himself to us. I've been completely undone many times as He has drawn me closer to Him. In 1993 a move of God began sweeping through Brisbane. I remember being initially very unsure about all the laughing and manifestations I saw. I remember praying, when I saw people laughing and running around the building under the power of the Holy Spirit, "God, protect me!"

But inwardly my heart burned with hunger for more of God. So I kept going to these "strange" meetings where I would cry while it seemed everyone around me was laughing. I was still really struggling with condemnation at that time, feeling terrible for weeks if I ever felt I let God down in any way at all. So I would go to nightly meetings where I would pour my heart out to God.

During this season I wrote a song to myself from God, reminding myself that God has covered our sin and taken our shame. It's one of the songs on my first album, *Faithful*. Soon after writing that song, I was at the altar again and had an amazing encounter with God. I found myself on the floor laughing and crying with deep, supernatural joy as I turned my face to see Jesus looking at me. His eyes were full of love for me. Seeing His eyes so full of love has changed me forever. He has overwhelmed me with His love and conveyed complete forgiveness with just a look.

He looks at you with just the same eyes. He longs to show His true feelings toward each of us. He wants us to know how much He adores us. He doesn't want just to reveal His love generally as part of His nature—as some theological principle—but personally as part of our experience. He wants it to sink deep into our hearts. The more I look, the more I see. God wants to write on the screen of your heart and show you how much He loves you.

We are blessed to have relationship with God. Within that relationship He means for us to have glorious encounters with Him and fellowship with Him in a very real way as He reveals Himself and His kingdom. God loves your company and wants to relate to you as His bride.

God is looking for those who will pursue a greater revelation of His love and find their identity there. These are the ones who will be able to believe Him with great faith. So many of His people are like the bride in the Song of Solomon: they hear Him calling them to come up higher, but they don't think they are ready. Perhaps His path seems a little extreme. They will gladly cheer Him on as He goes, but they don't take up the challenge to come away with Him to the heights. But they soon find that they aren't satisfied. They are restless. Their hearts long for Him. They can only be fulfilled with His love.

When we hear the Holy Spirit challenging us to come away with God to the heights of His love, our hearts need to respond. He is calling us to arise and shine. If we measure our ability to shine by our current performance, we'll never consider ourselves ready. But God isn't measuring us by our performance at all; He's calling us by our identity and our destiny. And our identity and destiny are completely in Him—in the depths of His unconditional love.

Seeing His eyes so full of love
has changed me forever.

This is where the spirit of wisdom and revelation will lead us. This is where we can begin to experience the One who is able to do immeasurably more than we can ask or think according to the power that works within us. This is the foundation of our relationship with Him and the goal of the apostolic prayers of Scripture. God wants us to be so rooted and grounded in love that it becomes our identity and the basis of all we do.

Chapter 3

DISCOVERING THE POWER OF IDENTITY

Who Does God Say You Are?

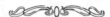

SEEING MYSELF AS a woman of dignity in heaven had a powerful effect on me. Not long after that encounter with God, I was asked to sing at a Full Gospel Businessmen's meeting. After I sang, a man got up to testify. He said he had prayed the prayer from Ephesians 3:14–21 every day for three months. He testified that during that time, he started to see angels joining him as he spent time with the Lord. In fact, he would even hear their footsteps coming up the path to his house. This really excited me, so I duly set about praying this prayer myself.

Every day I took this apostolic prayer and personalized it. I had enough faith to believe that when I asked anything according to God's will, He would give it to me. I knew that this prayer absolutely must be His will. How could it not be? It was in the Book and specifically written for all the saints. So every day I would kneel by my bed and pray this prayer. I wrote out a personalized version and even recorded it to play in the car as I drove.

I know I quoted the biblical version of this prayer from

Ephesians 3 earlier, but here's how I personalized it, with help from the Amplified Bible, as a prayer just between me and God:

For this reason I bow my knees before You, the Father of my Lord Jesus Christ, from whom every family in heaven and on earth is named. Grant me out of the rich treasury of Your glory to be strengthened with mighty power in my inner man by the [Holy] Spirit indwelling my innermost being [and personality]. May Christ through faith [actually] dwell in my heart! Help me to be rooted deep in love and founded securely on love, that I may have the power and be strong to apprehend and grasp with all the saints [God's devoted people, the experience of that love] what is the breadth and length and height and depth [of it]; [that I may really come] to know [practically, through experience for myself] the love of Christ, which far surpasses mere knowledge [without experience]; that I may be filled [through all my being] unto all the fullness of God [may I have the richest measure of the divine Presence, and become a body wholly filled and flooded with God Himself]! Now to You who, by the [action of His] power that is at work within us, is able to [carry out His purpose and] do superabundantly, far over and above all that I [dare] ask or think [infinitely beyond my highest prayers, desires, thoughts, hopes, or dreams]—to You

*be glory in the church and in Christ Jesus
throughout all generations forever and ever.
Amen (so be it).*

Little by little as I prayed, the revelation increased,
and soon it grew and began to crash over me with blissful
waves of joy. I still pray this prayer and encourage people
everywhere to do the same. It has changed my life to begin
to know how much He loves me.

One morning during my season of praying Ephesians
3, I woke up aware of God's powerful presence. As I lay in
bed worshipping, the weighty glory of God began to totally
overwhelm me with awe to the point that I was pinned
down and unable to speak. After a few minutes of speechless amazement I began to sing, without even thinking
about it, a spontaneous song to God as He gave me words
and melody:

> I kiss You with clean lips, O Lord,
> Lips that You've given to me,
> I kiss You with clean lips, O Lord,
> Because Your grace is sufficient for me.[1]

Then I was speechless again as God allowed the words
to sink into my heart. God had given me clean lips and a
pure heart! What a joy to know that we have been cleansed
from all guilt, shame, and condemnation. God wants us to
walk continuously in the glorious freedom He has bought
for us and to live without the weight of the condemning
voice of the accuser.

WHO DOES GOD SAY YOU ARE?

What our Father says about us is absolutely central to our ability to walk with Him in power. The name God gives us is so important for us to understand. That's why Paul prayed about every family deriving their name from the Father, and it's also why Jesus addresses the issue of identity too:

> Now when Jesus came into the district of Caesarea Philippi, He was asking His disciples, "Who do people say that the Son of Man is?" And they said, "Some say John the Baptist; and others, Elijah; but still others, Jeremiah, or one of the prophets." He said to them, "But who do you say that I am?" Simon Peter answered, "You are the Christ, the Son of the living God." And Jesus said to him, "Blessed are you, Simon Barjona, because flesh and blood did not reveal this to you, but My Father who is in heaven."
> —MATTHEW 16:13–17, NAS

Jesus asked His disciples who people were saying He was. They responded by saying some people thought He was John the Baptist, others Elijah, and others Jeremiah or one of the other prophets. But then Jesus wanted to know who His disciples thought He was. Peter answered correctly: "You are the Christ, the Son of the living God." Jesus rejoiced and said that the Father had given Peter a divine revelation. Peter's eyes had been supernaturally opened, as mine were on that day in worship when I was converted. The eyes of Peter's understanding were enlightened in the knowledge of God.

The personal revelation of Christ as Savior is the basis of salvation. It's a revelation that goes well beyond head knowledge—the enlightening of the eyes of your heart by the Holy Spirit. What really matters is who Christ is to you personally.

⁓⸿⤙⤚⸾⁓

What our Father says about us is absolutely central to our ability to walk with Him in power.

⸜⸿⤙⤚⸾⸜

But Jesus's conversation with His disciples didn't end with Peter's revelation. I love what happened next.

> And Jesus said to him, "Blessed are you, Simon Barjona, because flesh and blood did not reveal this to you, but My Father who is in heaven. I also say to you that you are Peter, and upon this rock I will build My church; and the gates of Hades will not overpower it. I will give you the keys of the kingdom of heaven; and whatever you bind on earth shall have been bound in heaven, and whatever you loose on earth shall have been loosed in heaven."
>
> —MATTHEW 16:17–19, NAS

Jesus addressed Peter by the name others knew him by—Simon Bar-Jonah. Simon means "reed-like" or "wavering," Bar-Jonah means "son of Jonas," and Jonas (among other things) can be translated as "wine-bibber." So, roughly translated, Simon Bar-Jonah can mean "unstable son of an alcoholic." Jesus was calling Peter by the name society knew him by, and it wasn't very flattering.

Many things in life try to define us. Who your parents are, whether you are rich or poor, how intelligent you are, what you have or haven't done, what you look like, your successes and your failures—all of these criteria help society form an opinion of who you are. Worse yet, we are often our own harshest critics, developing a self-perception that is based on our past failures, problems, and sins. Yet our true identity as believers is not defined by any of these things. We are defined by the fact that we are new creations in Christ. We bear the name the Father of our Lord Jesus Christ gives us.

Jesus was saying to Simon, "Society recognizes you as an unstable son of an alcoholic. But I have another revelation for you. I call you Peter." Peter, or *Petros* in Greek, means "a piece of rock." This is a glorious revelation. Jesus was showing Peter that he was made of the very same substance as the Rock, God Himself. Through Christ's body, wounded and pierced for us, we have been graciously grafted into the very DNA of God. We are part of the body of Christ! Just as water flowed from the rock that Moses struck, blood and water flowed from the side of Jesus the Rock. Just as Eve was formed out of Adam's side, Jesus's side was pierced and we have been created anew as His bride.

This relationship is beautifully portrayed in the Song of Songs:

> For you are My Dove,
> Hidden in the split open Rock.
> It was I who took you—
> And hid you up high
> In the secret stairway of the sky.
> Let Me see your radiant face

And hear your sweet voice.
How beautiful your eyes of worship,
How sweet and enchanting
Your voice in prayer,
For you are ravishing to Me!
—Song of Solomon 2:14, tpt

We have been hidden in the split-open side of Christ, the Rock! Or, as Colossians 3:3 says, "You died, and your life is hidden with Christ in God." So, through Jesus's death and resurrection, we have been created anew from the same substance as God Himself. We have become the righteousness of God in Christ. That's what Jesus was telling Peter—"As I am, so are you!" He has sanctified us and qualified us to be a suitable, perfect partner for God. It's a glorious and unfathomable mystery.

Then Jesus went on to say He would build His church on this rock—*Petra*, which is a different Greek word meaning "mass of rock," like Gibraltar. What did the Lord mean? I believe Jesus was saying that He would build His church on a twofold immovable rock of revelation—on the foundation of the revelation of who He is to you *and* who you are to Him.

One With Him

This is the unshakable foundation on which God wants to build His church. He says, "Listen to Me, you who follow after righteousness, you who seek the LORD: Look to the rock from which you were hewn" (Isa. 51:1). When you recognize and receive Christ as Savior, you become part of His body and receive a brand-new identity. You become the righteousness of God in Christ (2 Cor. 5:21). You have become one with Him. You are clothed in His glory. You and He are inseparable. As Christ is, so are you in this world (1 John 4:17).

Isaiah explains how this union came about:

> Surely He has borne our griefs and carried our sorrows; yet we esteemed Him stricken, smitten by God, and afflicted. But He was wounded for our transgressions, He was bruised for our iniquities; the chastisement for our peace was upon Him, and by His stripes we are healed. All we like sheep have gone astray; we have turned, every one, to his own way; and the LORD has laid on Him the iniquity of us all.
>
> —ISAIAH 53:4–6

Transgressions and *iniquities* are two different words. Transgressions refer to our sins, while iniquities in the Hebrew refers to our crookedness, our perverted nature. When sin entered the world through Adam and Eve, the nature of humanity became corrupted, which is why we are born with a sinful nature. Not only did Christ die for our sins, but He also died to deal with our corrupted nature and to give us the opportunity to be born again with His uncorrupted Spirit.

To have a revelation of Christ as your Savior is a wonderful thing, but without the revelation of what that means for you as a new creation, you can labor under the weight of a false identity. It's like trying to walk on one leg. To believe God wants to release healing through you, you must see yourself as He sees you! That's why Paul prays in Ephesians 1 that the eyes of our understanding would be enlightened both in the knowledge of Him *and* in the hope of our calling, the riches of the glory of His inheritance in the saints, and what is the exceeding greatness of His power toward us who believe. God wants to see you walking in the fullness of the revelation of His redemption so you can walk in the fullness of your call and His power.

Understanding who you are in Christ will enable you to walk with a confidence that is so powerful that not even the gates of Hades can prevail against it. God wants you to walk around with this incredible sense that "I am a gift, created to release the kingdom with power and to give Christ's joy, hope, and love to everyone I meet"—not because of what you've done but because of the value God has placed on you and the position He has put you in. The only effective weapon that the enemy has against believers is deception, and he works hard to keep the people of God from living out of their place of power.

He will undo you with His kindness.

Religious spirits will try to convince you that it is pride to think of yourself too highly. But to meditate on the reality of what Christ has done for you will only lead you to even greater humility. People get afraid that if they truly let this message sink into their heart, they will become proud, but it's not arrogance at all. The reality is that if you allow God to love you to the level that He wants to reveal His love to you, your heart won't say, "Oh, I'm so great." It will say, "Oh, God, You're so amazing!"

He will undo you with His kindness. His goodness and

kindness lead to repentance, not to arrogance. The more you let God tell you that you're special—that you have a destiny, you're going to change the world, and He's going to use you to bring His glory through you—and the more you step into your dreams and really believe them, the more humble you should become as you recognize, "Whoa, look what He's doing!" True humility enables us to receive with faith and gratitude what we know we haven't earned or deserved and releases us into a godly confidence that simply believes.

> We cannot earn the anointing. We must simply believe that we are coheirs with Christ.

The more I see God move in power through me, the more of Him I want and the more in awe of Him I become, knowing full well that the power has come because of His greatness and not through my works. It takes humility to receive what you can take no part in earning or deserving. If you could earn or deserve it, you could also take some of the glory for it. But God wants you to be so dependent on Him that there's no question where the power is coming from—and no question about who should receive glory for it. There's nothing we can do to earn His favor or to deserve the miracles He wants to perform through us. God steps through us as we nestle into His love. His miracle power is released when we believe Him and see Him do the work with the eyes of faith. Grace is a free gift, not an earned one.

The concept of earning grace has been a long-term

deception in the church. I mentioned how I used to fast for the whole day every time I was asked to preach, thinking that my fasting would increase the anointing—and the dilemma I faced when I started being asked to preach every day. Which services could I afford to be "less anointed" for? There's a place for fasting—I believe it increases our spiritual hunger—but when any form of spiritual discipline is used as a means of earning or qualifying yourself for something from God, it's similar to the prophets of Baal cutting themselves to get their god to do what they wanted. We cannot earn the anointing. We must simply believe that we are coheirs with Christ. In Him, as part of Him, we live and move and have our being (Acts 17:28).

YOU ALREADY HAVE
WHAT YOU NEED

A wonderful awakening is going on right now as the people of God are learning more and more to receive this truth by faith. Many are beginning to recognize the riches of our glorious inheritance, the greatness of God's power toward those who believe. People are realizing that they really are crucified with Christ and that He is living within them— and that they already have everything in Him. There's no need to strive for it or to feel the pain of falling short of it. It can't be earned or achieved. People are waking up and saying, "I'm actually free! That nagging torment that I'm not qualified is gone! My heart doesn't condemn me anymore!" And they are able to take hold of the promises God has given.

The enemy would love to trap us into thinking we must earn what Jesus has already done. That was Satan's trick in the very beginning. He told Adam and Eve, "You'll be like God if you eat the fruit of this tree." (See Genesis 3:4.) But remember what Scripture says about the way they were created? They had been made in God's image. They were already like Him! They fell into the trap of thinking, "If I grab hold of this fruit, then I can achieve something," yet they didn't realize that they already had what they were looking for. So do we. God doesn't want us to earn anything. He wants us to rest in Him and receive all that He is and all that He wants to give us.

God is looking for those who will recognize that they need to be utterly dependent on Him. In order to do this, we have to be secure in our identity. We have to believe what He says about us and get a vision of what He has promised us. If we know we are made of the same substance as God Himself, then we can confidently put all our hope in Him and let Him manifest His glory through us.

That doesn't mean faith doesn't do good works. We are created for good works in Christ, but the works don't come first. They earn nothing for us. They come out of a place of identity with Him. We *do* because we *are*. We don't do in order to become. A lot of believers are trying to do the works of the kingdom in order to become somebody significant in the kingdom. That's backward. It's an attempt to earn the authority God has already given. We don't have to become anything other than what we already are: people inhabited by God Himself and seated with Christ in heavenly realms. We heal the sick because we are filled with His Spirit. We give because we have a privileged position in heaven. We love because He first loved us. God wants us to do the works of the kingdom because we are already significant in the kingdom.

THE HEAVENLY MIRROR

> Prove yourselves doers of the word, and not
> merely hearers who delude themselves. For if
> anyone is a hearer of the word and not a doer,
> he is like a man who looks at his natural face in
> a *mirror*; for once he has looked at himself and
> gone away, he has immediately forgotten what
> kind of person he was.
>
> —JAMES 1:22–24, NAS,
>
> emphasis added

This passage used to make me feel condemned. I would think about how far I was from fully doing all that the Word said. Yet this is not what James is saying at all. He says if you are not doing the Word—that is, manifesting the character and power of Jesus through your life—it is because you have forgotten what you look like. God wants to remind us of our identity, and that comes by beholding Him. "We all, with unveiled face, beholding as in a *mirror* the glory of the Lord, are being transformed into the same image from glory to glory, just as from the Lord, the Spirit" (2 Cor. 3:18, NAS, emphasis added). As we behold God and seek to know Him, everything we discover about His character and power is as a mirror to us, reminding us of what we look like! The Bible tells us that when we are born again, it is no longer we who live but Christ who lives in us. In knowing Him, we are reminded of our identity.

Peter puts it this way:

> His divine power has granted to us everything
> pertaining to life and godliness, through the
> true knowledge of Him who called us by His

own glory and excellence. For by these He has granted to us His precious and magnificent promises, so that by them you may become partakers of the divine nature, having escaped the corruption that is in the world by lust. Now for this very reason also, applying all diligence, in your faith supply moral excellence, and in your moral excellence, knowledge, and in your knowledge, self-control, and in your self-control, perseverance, and in your perseverance, godliness, and in your godliness, brotherly kindness, and in your brotherly kindness, love. For if these qualities are yours and are increasing, they render you neither useless nor unfruitful in the true knowledge of our Lord Jesus Christ. For he who lacks these qualities is blind or short-sighted, having *forgotten* his purification from his former sins.

—2 PETER 1:3–9, NAS,
emphasis added

It's so important to realize
you *are* before you *do.*

Everything pertaining to life and godliness has been given to us, and we activate it all through the supernatural knowledge of what God is like. If we aren't manifesting these qualities and the nature and power Christ in our lives, it is because we have forgotten our true identity.

God speaks so kindly to me when I am alone with Him. Just a few words from Him can cut through whatever anxieties I may have and give me supernatural peace. But it is in knowing how His voice makes me feel that I am reminded that I too have the power to bring that sort of peace to others with my words. In fact, everything I discover about God in the Bible and through fellowship with Him also serves as a mirror to me, reminding me that this is what I now look like as a child of God. As I seek to know Him, I discover who I am and the power that I now have to do the work of the kingdom.

We will take a closer look later at what it means to get to know God, but know for now that the foundation of seeking His face is knowing the truth of who He is and who you are in Him—finding your identity in His love. There is absolutely *nothing* for you to do to obtain that identity, but everything you do should come from that place of security. It's so important to realize you *are* before you *do*. And you can only know who you are as you receive a revelation of His deep, relentless love.

Chapter 4

FAITH ROOTED IN LOVE

Free to Receive, Qualified to Give

SOON AFTER MY deliverance the Lord spoke to me and called me into full-time ministry. I was twenty-three at the time, and though the calling wouldn't manifest for several more years, I began to have visions of myself preaching while fireballs went out over the crowds healing the sick and bringing people to salvation. There were days when I couldn't get up off the floor as I groaned with what seemed like birth pangs in the presence of God. I would wake up with open visions and with my heart breaking for the lost but also overflowing with joy at how the Lord wanted to use me. He was giving me His heart. His voice had become so clear, and I knew I was being called to preach.

"TRUST GOD, SISTER!"

Even though I believed God, I didn't know how this calling could become a reality. It seemed so ridiculous, so unlikely. I didn't know how to prepare because I couldn't see any clear path into this destiny. And at the time I knew of hardly any women who were in ministry. I remember coming across Maria Woodworth-Etter's *Diary of Signs and Wonders* and being undone as I read her story. Here she was, a housewife complaining to God that she was not qualified for the work. I knew exactly how she felt. But the Lord continued to confirm the call to me in so many wonderful ways, even telling Tom about it before I did. The calling was very clear.

Despite all of this, I decided that what I really needed was a prophet to pick me out of a crowd and declare the call on my life. That would confirm it for me. I figured that with a strong prophetic word given to me from the pulpit, the pastor and my family would all have to accept this as my destiny and perhaps even help me with it. So when the next prophetic minister came to our church for a series of meetings, I was ready. I explained to God that I was a woman and therefore needed special help if I was going to do what He was asking. It made perfect sense to me that He would be willing to publicly confirm what I already knew privately.

The meetings started. On the first night the prophet called several people out of the crowd, and it was just as if he had read their mail. I was so excited, hoping it would be my turn next! But the meeting ended, and I hadn't received a word. A little deflated, I went to the altar at the end of the service to give God another chance. The man made his way down the line, prophesying people's destinies, and then finally he got to me. I took a deep breath and prepared for him to affirm my destiny for all to hear. "Trust God, sister!" he said. That was it. Then he moved on to the next person.

I was so upset. Where was the rest of the prophecy? Where was the confirmation I was looking for? I wanted so badly to ask him if he had seen anything else. Surely he had forgotten something! That couldn't be all God wanted him to say to me.

The next night was the last night of ministry, so during the day I became very serious with God in my prayer time. I told Him, "Unless You have the prophet call me out tonight and declare my destiny, I will give it all up as my imagination." Despite the visions, despite feeling God's heartbeat for the lost, and despite the fact that my husband could see the calling on my life, I was willing to put it all on the line. So I sat through the meeting that night with bated breath. With so much at stake, surely God would speak.

The ministry began, and people were being called out and prophesied over. God was speaking His will into the lives of His people. I waited expectantly, but nothing came. Then the altar was opened for anyone else wanting prayer. I felt distraught that somehow I had been forgotten, so I went to the altar and waited for my word. Finally the preacher came to me, put his hands on my head, and declared, "Trust God, sister!"

Even if no one ever prophesies it, I choose to believe
what the Holy Spirit has revealed to my heart.

I burst into tears. Some of my friends saw me crying and obviously felt sorry for me, so they went and got the prophet's helper to come and pray for me. He didn't get any revelations about my destiny either. There were no words about my calling to ministry. He said only that he felt my husband needed to take me on a vacation! I just cried all the more.

I went home a blubbering mess and threw myself on the bed with my Bible. I flung it open and demanded that God speak to me. Mercifully it opened at the Book of Luke, and I read this:

> There was a man in Jerusalem whose name was Simeon, and this man was just and devout, waiting for the Consolation of Israel, and the Holy Spirit was upon him. And it had been revealed to him by the Holy Spirit that he would not see death before he had seen the Lord's Christ. So he came by the Spirit into the temple. And when the parents brought in the Child Jesus, to do for Him according to the custom of the law, he took Him up in his arms and blessed God and said: "Lord, now You are letting Your servant depart in peace, according to Your word."
>
> —LUKE 2:25–29

As I read of the Holy Spirit revealing to Simeon's heart that he would see the Messiah before he died, I was cut to the heart with conviction. The Spirit had spoken to my heart, and I had said it wasn't enough. I realized that Simeon had simply believed, even though it was never prophesied to him, and I knew the Lord was speaking to me to do the same. I was simply to believe what He had told me. That should have been enough. That's what the prophet meant when he said, "Trust God, sister!"

I got down beside my bed and began to pray. I declared out loud what I had been too scared to accept—that even if no one ever prophesies it, I choose to believe what the Holy Spirit has revealed to my heart. Even with no one else in the room to hear me, it seemed hard to say it out loud, but still I declared that God was calling me to preach the gospel, to go to the nations, and to heal the sick. He had already spoken, I had heard Him accurately, He had confirmed it, and all that was left was to believe. So I made the choice to receive that call with joy and faith.

ONLY BELIEVE

Several years after that decision to accept God's words to me by faith, I became something of a prophecy magnet. He began to confirm again and again what I had already accepted. Whenever I went to meetings, the speakers would pick me out of the crowd and prophesy that I was called to go to the nations to heal the sick and preach. Now, deep within my heart, I was able to quietly and confidently say, "I know." Though it was another seven years before I began to see the fulfillment of this promise, it had become solid in my heart ever since the night I had declared it beside my bed.

If God had done as I had demanded and given me a prophetic word when I wanted it, I would have adopted that as a pattern—always waiting for a word from someone else before making any major decisions in my life. I would have put my future into the hands of other people's obedience and would have missed so many opportunities. I would have been reluctant to act on anything I had heard directly from God myself. I had to learn a foundational truth: only believe!

MIRACLES DISPLAY
GOD'S FAITHFULNESS

Healings and miracles give God glory, and we must believe God wants to use us! I remember one night in Augusta, Georgia, when the Lord gave me a word of knowledge about someone who had a deaf ear. It was the first word of knowledge I received that evening, so everyone was listening expectantly. I had seen a number of deaf ears open before, so the word itself didn't surprise me. But I didn't expect what was about to happen with this one. A woman who had no ear came forward. Her ear had been surgically removed because of a tumor. She had always tried to cover the absence of her ear with her hair.

My heart sank as she stood before me at the front of this Methodist church. As we talked, I found out that not only did she have no ear, but also the eardrum was gone. I was hoping to see God perform a miracle to build everyone's faith and confirm the Word that had just been preached. Standing before her, I felt that the best I could hope for was that she would grow an eardrum back overnight. I had seen God restore deaf ears, but I felt that for God to give hearing when there was no ear, let alone no eardrum, would take more faith than I had.

Nevertheless, this beautiful woman stood there in faith, believing that God would restore her hearing. So I proceeded. I shared with her a testimony of a woman in Australia whom I had prayed for. She said she had been born without an eardrum and had received healing. After I shared this story, I went to lay my right hand on her, trying not to feel too intimidated by the missing ear. My right hand often trembles when the anointing is flowing

56

through me—it's always an encouraging sign to me—and I have seen God do remarkable miracles as I have laid my trembling hand on people. But as I went to lay my right hand on this woman, the Lord spoke and said, "Put your left hand on her."

I was a little perturbed by this instruction, as I felt that my faith needed the extra support that night. "Lord, this is a serious case here!" I told Him. "I need all the help I can get. I feel the anointing in my right hand, and I don't feel anything in my left."

"Put your left hand on her," He said again.

"OK, Lord." I've learned that God is actually a good bit smarter than I am, so I did what He said. But I didn't feel like anything happened when I put my left hand on her and prayed.

"Ask her if she can hear," He nudged.

So I whispered into this ear—or rather this place where the ear and the eardrum had been physically cut out—very quietly. "Can you hear me?"

"Yes!" the woman yelled as she swung her head around. "I can hear!" And I think I might have been more shocked than she was.

That miracle caused the level of faith in the congregation to rise, and many more received healing. I went home quite tired, having prayed for people late into the night. As I climbed the stairs to my bedroom, I began to think about the excitement of the people. I knew they would come back the next night with all their sick friends and with great expectations for similar healings. Suddenly I began to feel the weight of the level of their expectation, and I was a bit concerned. It seemed to me that the bar had been raised, and I began to feel more than a little intimidated by what the Lord had done. What if the anointing wasn't as strong the next night? Would people become disappointed?

I had left my laptop playing in my room on "shuffle," and as I climbed the stairs that night, one of Kathryn Kuhlman's little heart-to-heart talks was playing. I could hear her lilting voice saying that every time she walked out onto the platform, she would die a thousand deaths, knowing that there were people in the congregation who had come to the miracle service as their last hope. I had heard her say that before, but tonight, for the first time, I felt I understood. She went on to say she encouraged herself with the knowledge that everything Jesus did on the earth, He did as a man, utterly dependent on the Holy Ghost. "And the Holy Spirit never let Him down," she continued. And then to my amazement, in her slow, melodic voice she said, "And the Holy Spirit will never let *you* down."[1]

My time of need is still all the time!

I felt like God had kissed me! Knowing how much He loves me empowers me to trust Him. The next night another deaf ear opened and more arthritis was healed. And the following night, as if to make a point, God opened another deaf ear, and the miracles continued to flow.

FREE TO RECEIVE, QUALIFIED TO GIVE

The Holy Spirit is still my ever-present help in time of need. And my time of need is still all the time! I utterly depend on Him, and He continually unfolds to me more truth about His amazing love, empowering me to trust Him and expect miracles. And this is available to all who believe. Truly we are the apple of His eye, His favorite ones!

> I truly am the rose of His heart,
> The very theme of His song!
> I'm His ever-fresh lily growing even in the
> valley!
> —SONG OF SOLOMON 2:1, TPT

The love of God is the answer to all the fears that hold us back from receiving His goodness. I remember a night when I was conducting a crusade in Australia, and a woman came forward for prayer. She had been to the meetings for three nights and had hovered around at the back, too ashamed to sit closer to the front during the meeting. On the very last night she finally came forward for prayer. The Holy Spirit did something very powerful in her life as she lay trembling on the floor after being delivered and set free. I had the privilege of leading her to Christ while she was on the floor that night.

A few days later I received a letter from her that touched my heart. She said since that service she had not been able to smoke an entire cigarette because she would choke on any puff she'd take. But that wasn't the most exciting thing. She had been abused as a child and had lived on the streets since she was ten years old. When she came to the service, she was addicted to heroin and working as a prostitute, but after the Lord touched her, she stopped using drugs and experienced no withdrawal symptoms. She was miraculously set free.

This precious lady rang up all her suppliers the day

after her deliverance and told them to stay away from her because she had been born again. She then went out and met another addict on the street and told him and his girlfriend what had happened to her and how she was "off the stuff." He responded that if God would do something about his stomach that was really giving him trouble, he would believe her. So my precious friend, saved for less than twenty-four hours, offered to pray for him.

She laid her hands on his belly, and the man was slain in the Spirit on the sidewalk. When he got up out of the bushes, he was speechless with amazement. He reached into his pocket and pulled out five hundred dollars and gave it to my friend, which was great because she now had decided to give up "work." He also gave three hundred dollars to his girlfriend and told both of them, "That's what I would have spent on heroin this week. I'm not going to need it now!"

No one had told this woman that she should have waited until she had been through a course or been approved by the elders before laying hands on people in the street. Like the woman at the well who ran off to tell the whole town about her encounter with God, she wanted to share what she had received.

That's what we are told to do. "Freely you have received, freely give" (Matt. 10:8). God has rooted and grounded us in His love, and He has also called us to give His love away to others. After Paul tells us we have become new creations in Christ, he tells us that just as we have been reconciled to God, we are to be ministers of reconciliation to bring people to God. He has committed to us the word of reconciliation, not of judgment. In other words, we are to tell people how deeply God loves them and wants them to come to Him. We let them know how wide, how long, how deep, and how high God's amazing love really is. That's our calling, and everyone who has received His love is qualified to give it away.

DECLARE HIS FAITHFULNESS

I opened this chapter by telling you about the times when I first sensed God calling me into a ministry of speaking and seeing people healed and saved how He put His heart within me for the things He wanted me to do. What I didn't tell you was that He gave me a promise at the time: "In your thirtieth year I'm going to open a door for you into full-time ministry." I was twenty-three, so it would take seven years for things to unfold. I was excited because I had read that both Joseph and Jesus began their public ministries at the age of thirty. But when my thirtieth year came, I was doing less in ministry than I ever had been. It seemed like even the few opportunities I did have were taken away. I was pregnant with my youngest child, depressed, and confused about God's call. It was one of the lowest points in my life.

During that season I had two close friends die of cancer, and I had prayed for them both. One night soon after the second friend's death, I remember being in a worship service, and in my grief I tried to put the healing ministry in the "too-hard" basket. (I'll share more about this in chapter 7.) I figured it was safer just to preach salvation and to prophesy, as it seemed that telling people that God still performed miracles was too risky.

I didn't want to raise hope in people if they weren't going to be healed. As I was talking with God about this,

I had one of the most significant encounters I had ever had. In an open vision God spoke to me and simply said, "You must believe." It was so significant that it settled the matter for me, despite what happened with my friends and what I saw in my natural circumstances. I determined to trust God. He tells us to heal the sick and declare that the kingdom of God has come upon them. Since then we have seen many healed of cancer. We cannot change or water down the gospel.

Like the twelve spies sent into the Promised Land, we have a choice as to whether we see the problem or the promise. Ten came back and said that the problems were insurmountable. Two, Joshua and Caleb, focused on the faithfulness of God's promise. Of all who were offered the promise, only these two inherited it through faith and patience. They were determined not to let circumstances determine what they believed.

Nine days before I turned thirty-one, I remembered the promise. "Lord, when I was twenty-three, You said You were going to open the door to ministry in my thirtieth year," I prayed. "There are nine days left. You said it, and I'm picking it up and believing it." And I began to declare God's faithfulness and went to war with that promise. I clung to a passage in 1 Timothy:

> This command I entrust to you, Timothy, my son, in accordance with the prophecies previously made concerning you, that by them you fight the good fight, keeping faith and a good conscience, which some have rejected and suffered shipwreck in regard to their faith.
> —1 TIMOTHY 1:18–19, NAS

As I battled with this word, I sensed God telling me to
go to a conference that was going on at the time. So I got
up and went that day and sat next to a woman who, as it
turns out, happened to be a respected prophet and a traveling minister. She invited me to lunch, and as we talked,
she said she felt that the Lord was telling her to mentor me.

We have a choice as to whether we see the problem or the promise.

"I'd like to train you up, take you with me when I minister, and help you develop the gift of God on your life,"
she said.

"Hooray!" I thought to myself. And I experienced God's
faithfulness and an open door nine days before I turned
thirty-one—just as He promised. (This woman's example
has shaped my own passionate desire to do for others as
she did for me. For this reason I regularly take interns
with me as I travel. We all need to be discipling others and
raising up the next generation.)

I strongly believe in waging war with the faithfulness
of God as our weapon, declaring His faithfulness, even
when we don't understand what is going on. The title track
from my first album is called "Faithful," and I penned it as
a declaration during this time when it seemed as though
nothing was happening. Just as David wrote many of his
psalms in the wilderness, many of my songs came out of
this time. Declaring my hope in God was and still is one of
my most effective battle strategies.

We don't need to step into our own fight; we can rest

in what He has promised and let Him wage our battles for us. His faithfulness is our shield. When He has called us, He will also open the doors that make the fulfillment possible. His love not only gives us our identity, but it also shows us our destiny—*and* leads us into it. When we are rooted and grounded in the love that passes all our understanding, we can confidently believe Him and boldly step into the plans He has for us.

Chapter 5

SPENDING TIME IN HIS PRESENCE

"Yummy Daddy Time"

I RECEIVED A PHONE call one day from Gareth Barnes, one of the young pastors Tom and I have had the privilege to mentor. I had just recently finished preaching a series on enjoying time with God, and he greeted me on the phone that day with the comment, "Have you had your yummy Daddy time today?" His wording so struck me that I remember saying to a friend who was with me that we really should be using that as a Christian greeting!

When you have a revelation of how much God enjoys seeing you every day, time with Him becomes a delight, not a chore. And a question like "Have you had yummy Daddy time today?" can be taken as an enticing suggestion rather than a religious checkup. I have become so addicted to fellowship with God that I find I need time alone with Him more than I need food. I love food and would graze all day if I could, but without continuously enjoying God's presence, I feel spiritually famished and tired. When it comes to God, I need three meals a day plus snacks!

I remember once being at an altar and crying out to

God that I was so needy for love, and He gave me a vision. I saw a deep, jagged cut in me. Then I saw a jagged piece that was shaped to fit exactly into the very deepest parts of the cut. It came down from heaven and completely filled the gap. It was a perfect fit in every corner of my life. This was how God showed me that He will love us to the level of our deepest need.

> When it comes to God, I need three
> meals a day plus snacks!

The more you understand your need, the more you discover that He is able to fill up the empty places. But He doesn't just want to fill you up; He wants you to over-flow. Our greatest joy is to be lavishly loved by God and to overflow with love. God, who is love, created us as His counterpart, in His image, to have a love relationship more glorious than anything ever conceived. Brian Simmons, a Bible translator and dear friend of ours, has recently trans-lated the Song of Songs capturing the Hebrew dynamic equivalent of the text. It is called the *Passion Translation*, and I've quoted it several times throughout this book.

Look how he has translated this passage from chapter 4, where the Bridegroom King, our Lord, rejoices over us His bride:

> My beloved one, My equal, My bride.
> I am undone by your love.
> Merely a glance
> From your worshipping eyes
> And you have stolen my heart.

Just gazing into your heart,
Joined to Mine,
And I am overcome!
Conquered! Ravished!
Held hostage by your love!
How satisfying to Me, My equal, My beautiful
  bride.
Your love is My finest wine,
Intoxicating and thrilling—
And your sweet praise—perfume
So exotic, so pleasing.
Your loving words are like honey to Me,
Drenched with worship.
                    —SONG OF SOLOMON 4:9–11, TPT

This is such a stunning thought, that we affect God's heart so powerfully. God doesn't have a "take it or leave it" attitude about our love; He loves with greater emotion than you and I have ever come close to experiencing. We are His soft spot, the very apple of His eye. And He is deeply touched by our worship. Our highest call is to minister to Him. We love because He first loved us. We cannot give what we do not first receive, so God is always waiting to give us more and invites us to a never-ending love feast.

As I'm writing this, I am on a plane from London to Los Angeles. Every time I get on a plane, the same announcement is made, no matter which airline I am traveling on. They tell you that if an oxygen mask is released, you must put it on yourself first and breathe, and only then are you to help others around you, including any children. That always seemed rather selfish to me because your first instinct, especially as a mother, is to look after your children. But I soon realized that you would not be much use to your children or anyone else if you were unconscious. In the same way, we need to daily breathe in the oxygen of God's love as our highest priority if we are to be fruitful. Without love I am nothing. God wants us to overflow, and overflow requires constant filling!

We are His soft spot,
the very apple of His eye.

When you are feeding on the Word of God and living in His love, there is a clarity in your life that allows other people to see what's inside you—the power of God. I believe that when God's people have this kind of clarity—when we are pure, clean, and obsessed with Jesus—the Holy Spirit's power will show up with greater healings and wonders. I've recently been discovering a deliverance ministry I didn't know I had. I used to think it was a specialized field, but as I've become more focused and aware of having Jesus inside of me, deliverance just happens spontaneously. Darkness flees when you have the light of the world and the power of God living inside of you.

That's why it bothers me when someone criticizes others for being "too heavenly minded to be any earthly good." How are you going to be any earthly use if you're not completely heavenly minded? To be heavenly minded is to be fixated on things above and things that are praiseworthy and pure and lovely. It is sad when people mock someone for being "super-spiritual"—as though they aren't being "real." How can we *not* be completely absorbed in who God is and what He is doing in this world? How can we *not* fully pursue His purity and His glory? We aren't of this world anymore. We function in this world, but we really live in a heavenly realm. And in that realm we get our life, our energy, and our strength from being saturated in God's love. That's how we impact the world. That's what makes it possible for us to show others His love. Without abiding in and drinking of the river of His great pleasure for us, we can't love others as we should. The kingdom of God is righteousness, peace, and joy, and God wants to help us continually emanate the things of His kingdom.

Knowing that God loves me allows me to approach Him with great confidence. I know now that whether I have spent much time fellowshipping with Him or not, He is always eager to pick up right where we left off without making me feel even one little bit of condemnation. His look of delight is pure and untainted. Such love convicts me and draws me away after Him with ever-increasing adoration and amazement.

POSITIONING YOURSELF FOR LOVE

The Book of Jude was written to Christians who were dealing with a lot of distractions: false teaching, divisive words, complaining, and more. So Jude says, "But you, beloved, building yourselves up on your most holy faith, praying in the Holy Spirit, keep yourselves in the love of God, waiting anxiously for the mercy of our Lord Jesus Christ to eternal life" (Jude 20–21, NAS). These are keys to keep us on the right course.

What does it mean to keep yourself in the love of God? It certainly can't mean that His love is still undecided about you, so you'd better not lose it. His love doesn't change toward you. It is intense and powerful. Regardless of what you've done or how you feel about Him, He still loves you just the same. He loves you completely. He always has, and He always will. There is nothing any of us can do to earn God's love or to forfeit it. So to keep yourself in His love can't mean to maintain His love and make sure you don't lose it.

No, Jude is talking about positioning yourself to receive God's love—to experience it at a practical level. There's a war going on for your attention. God wants to see your face—to see your eyes gazing at Him, to lift your countenance, to make you shine, to fill you up with love so you can give His love to the "unlovely" of this world. He wants you to be completely absorbed in Him so you can come into union with Him and walk in the power of the Holy Spirit, loving and forgiving and being a catalyst for signs and wonders. When you overflow with His love, miracles begin to happen all around you.

But the enemy is always trying to distract you and redirect your focus to all kinds of hassles and problems. He wants to fill your mind and heart with disturbing thoughts and feelings. He wants to get your attention and turn your face toward anything or anyone other than God. He wants to see you frown, get discouraged, and approach life with fear, which is the opposite of faith. Not only will this keep you from experiencing intimacy with God, but it will also keep you from doing the works of heaven.

So to keep yourself in the love of God is to deliberately position yourself where you can keep your focus on God and receive the love He wants to show you. And you really do have to be very deliberate about it because the distractions can be quite persistent and intense. Time is the new money, and in this world of e-mail, Facebook, Twitter, and mobile phones, it is easily spent. I need time alone with God to drink in His love and allow Him to restore my soul more than I need anything else. I need much more than just one focused time alone with Him a day. His love is my life source, and I want to live overflowing with His love. Faith works by love, and God *is* love, so it is in His love that we are to live and move and have our being. To do that, we must learn to drink deeply, deliberately, and continuously from the river of His pleasure that flows with love for us. And we need more than just a sip, because God wants us to thrive, not just survive. We have the privilege of being infused with supernatural strength and joy, so drink deeply!

As Jude's instruction implies, there's a link between praying in the Holy Spirit, building ourselves up in faith, and keeping ourselves in the love of God. As we pray in the Spirit, the Holy Spirit enlarges our capacity to receive love and strengthens us so we can supernaturally comprehend it. He prays through us with power, cutting through clouds of confusion that the enemy tries to blind us with. As we pray in tongues, the Holy Spirit prays through us and for us about things that are not naturally seen, going before us and making our paths straight. He knows what we need to pray about and helps us in our weakness with perfect intercession. He unfolds mysteries to us. Revelation is downloaded into our hearts, and the gifts are stirred up.

But you have to come before God knowing He *will* give, not in a vain hope that He *might* provide what you need from Him. If He commanded you to keep yourself in His love, then He will keep His end of the deal. Sometimes people come to Him hoping that He might give them the breakthrough they are looking for or do something that proves He's on their side. But we already know these things. We come to Him in faith knowing that He is a rewarder of those who seek Him (Heb. 11:6). When you come with a deliberate understanding that the command of God is to keep yourself in His love, you can come with the full expectation that His love *will* be shed abroad in your heart by the Spirit.

This is like getting a hug from God. It's like a child holding his arms out and saying, "Here I am—up, Daddy!" God can't resist that. He says, "Oh, I love you so much!" That's the childlike certainty we can bring to Him. We just go and get it. There's no question that our Daddy will pick us up and show us His love. When we bask in the intense power of His love, we can't help but be changed. Just as you can't sunbathe and not get hot, you can't come into God's presence and not be affected by the warmth of His love. That's why I call it "yummy Daddy time." It's just wonderful.

Life will get filled with busyness and distractions, and when that happens, you have to be even more deliberate about keeping yourself in His presence. The enemy will try everything he can to keep you away from it, and even good things can become the enemy of the best. But I've found that I'm too busy *not* to pray. Intimate fellowship with God through prayer is the key to fruitfulness. I like having time with people, but I *must* have my time with God. I must have my time in the sunshine of His presence, having quality time with Him where He lifts me up and refreshes me and renews my strength, just as He promised. If I don't, my battery runs out.

I've been in conferences that were filled with meetings

morning, afternoon, and night, and there hasn't been much time to be alone with God. I've realized that after a couple of days of that, I have to risk being rude and tell my hosts that if I'm not speaking during a particular session, I need to be excused or leave early because I have to spend some time alone with God. I love corporate worship times and really don't like to miss any opportunities for the refreshing they bring, and I love to listen to great speakers, but I still need quality time alone in the secret place every day.

> ### When we bask in the intense power of His love, we can't help but be changed.

I get desperate for Daddy time! I used to be judgmental toward speakers for not showing up at every session, thinking they were arrogant for not coming to all the conference sessions. But now I'm one of them! I have to guard my time with God; if I don't have enough time alone with Him, I have nothing worth giving. When I'm given time to talk with God and my family, and to sleep eight hours, I stay happy and healthy and fruitful.

You need to have this time too. In the midst of all the distractions in your life and the ways the enemy tries to keep you from fulfilling your calling, you must position yourself to experience God's love. As you pray in the Spirit and build yourself up in faith, the Spirit will stir you up so you can't help but want to seek God's face more. And as you keep yourself in God's love, you'll have the anointing and wisdom you need to bring people into His kingdom. He is everything we need.

I have now learned to very intentionally schedule time into my day when I can just take the time to be loved. I try not to schedule appointments before 10:30 in the morning, as I need time to be alone with God. I love to walk with God, as being outside alone with Him without the distractions of phones or people is so refreshing. I have heard missionary Heidi Baker say that she goes snorkeling to get alone with God. At least underwater you can't hear the phones ringing, and people would have to make a big effort to get to you! I understand this now because time with God is my lifeline, where I am refreshed and strengthened for the work.

~୧୫ ୬୬ ୬ ~

Intimacy is the key to fruitfulness.

୬ ୧୫ ୬ ୬

Even Jesus needed this time. He would climb mountains and find solitary places to be alone. This was His vital connection with the Father. With the constant demands of ministry, Jesus understood the "one thing" that was most important (Ps. 27:4). He showed us by example that we all need to do whatever it takes to spend quality time alone with God. As humans we need sleep and food to renew our physical strength. In the same way, we need "yummy Daddy time" just as regularly to stay strong spiritually. And I have discovered that when I am strong spiritually, I also feel physically strong. In God's presence there is fullness of joy, and His joy is my strength. The prophet Isaiah tells us:

He gives power to the weak, and to those who
have no might He increases strength. Even the
youths shall faint and be weary, and the young
men shall utterly fall, but those who wait on
the LORD shall renew their strength; they shall
mount up with wings like eagles, they shall run
and not be weary, they shall walk and not faint.

—ISAIAH 40:29–31

You can see how important it is to have time alone
with God. Whatever it takes, make sure you get it! So
much happens during this time. We get happy, and our
souls are restored. We also become familiar with His voice
and His Presence. God wants fellowship with us, and the
more we fellowship with Him, the stronger our faith in
Him becomes. Intimacy is the key to fruitfulness.

I will often walk in the garden with God, talking to
Him as people would talk with a friend. The wonderful
thing about being with God is that, unlike human friends,
He understands me completely. There's no need to explain
myself. Spending time with the One who really knows
me and utterly loves me is my favorite thing to do. There
have been times when I have been going through difficulties, and in those times I have just felt the Father put His
arm around me as we walked and talked, reducing me to
tears with His affection and care. Other times I will just
sit in my bedroom with Him, without an agenda, and He
surprises and delights me with the things He shares from
His heart.

PURE, LOVELY, AND
OF A GOOD REPORT

The Father is so much kinder than we have ever understood. He doesn't want us to live with anxiety. Anxiety has its base in fear, and fear brings torment, but His perfect love casts out fear. Instead of being anxious, the Lord tells us to talk with Him about our concerns and ask for help, thanking Him for being faithful to work it all out for the good of those who love Him and are called according to His purpose (Rom. 8:28). After laying the weight of our anxieties on Him, we are encouraged to rest in the truth that He hears us and will answer our prayers.

Paul assured the members of the Philippian church that they could completely trust God, let go of their anxiety, and fill their hearts and minds with peaceful, comforting thoughts:

> Be anxious for nothing, but in everything by
> prayer and supplication, with thanksgiving,
> let your requests be made known to God; and
> the peace of God, which surpasses all understanding, will guard your hearts and minds
> through Christ Jesus. Finally, brethren, whatever things are true, whatever things are noble,
> whatever things are just, whatever things
> are pure, whatever things are lovely, whatever things are of good report, if there is any
> virtue and if there is anything praiseworthy—
> meditate on these things. The things which you
> learned and received and heard and saw in me,
> these do, and the God of peace will be with you.
> —PHILIPPIANS 4:6–9

To enter into this peaceful rest, we are told to think about things that are pure and lovely and of a good report. In other words, if the thought is not pure, lovely, or praiseworthy, it doesn't belong in our brain. Colossians says to "set your minds and keep them set on what is above" (Col. 3:2, AMP). God wants to fill our hearts and minds with heavenly thinking, not judgment and negativity. An old Sunday school chorus says, "Be careful, little eyes, what you see...be careful, little ears, what you hear..." We must guard our hearts and minds! What gets your attention gets you.

My mother used to say, "Meddle with tar, and it will stick to you," and she is right. Bad company corrupts good character, and ugly conversation and entertainment contaminates pure thinking and erodes your peace. You cannot fill your mind with entertainment involving immorality and violence and at the same time keep your mind set on praiseworthy things. Similarly judgment, negativity, and criticism poison our hearts. We are invited to enter into the rest of faith and swat like flies the rogue thoughts that would try to steal our peace.

If I am being troubled by worries or rogue thoughts when I go to pray or worship, my natural reaction is to condemn myself for not having enough discipline over those thoughts. But I've learned to stop doing that. Instead I try to catch those thoughts and recognize they are things that I have not yet released to God in order to get His help with them. After all, perhaps those thoughts have come up for a reason. If you have a similar battle with stray thoughts when you pray, try to identify why they are coming up. If they are issues that haven't been dealt with, release them to God for Him to take care of. It may even be that the

Holy Spirit is trying to bring things to your attention that you need to pray about.

Once you have "caught all the flies" like this, the air becomes clear and you can start to hear the heart of God. This is where prophetic intercession begins. Having cleared your heart and mind through prayer and petition, having cast your cares on Him, you can rest in faith and begin to hear what is on God's heart. You may begin to hear Him speak. As you do, declare what He says out loud, agreeing with heaven so it is established on earth. You may have visions and be taken to places in the Spirit so that you can see things happening that God wants you to pray about. Dealing with His business can be glorious fun! God loves to share His heart with you and involve you in His kingdom business.

Prayer times can be a little like the relationship between a husband and wife. Both need to communicate requests concerning the mundane issues of life. ("Would you mind taking the children to school?" "Can you pay this bill?" and so on.) But once all the business of the day is taken care of, then it's time to move beyond requests and begin to build a healthy relationship. Investing in a relationship takes time for both parties to just relax and enjoy each other's company and have times of intimate conversation with each other. So it is with God. He wants you to talk with Him and bring Him your requests, but He also wants you to share your heart and talk about your passions and enjoy His company. And He wants to tell you about His kingdom and about His business and passions too. He wants to have intimate fellowship with you through which you can receive love and return it to Him as well. We call that worship.

I used to struggle with the concept of worship. As a child I wondered why God would want us to tell Him how good He is all the time. Wasn't Jesus the picture of humility? Why did He need to be praised? I didn't understand that worship is actually lover's talk. We come to Him like little children with upraised arms or as lovers with outstretched arms ready for a hug. He responds by embracing us and telling us how much we are loved. Our hearts respond in awe and amazement, and the love flows in beautiful worship.

THE RESPONSE OF LOVE

When Jesus encountered the woman at a well, the conversation eventually turned to God's desire for worship.

> An hour is coming, and now is, when the true worshipers will worship the Father in spirit and truth; for such people the Father seeks to be His worshipers. God is spirit, and those who worship Him must worship in spirit and truth.
> —JOHN 4:23–24, NAS

The Father was looking forward to the day when His children could freely come to Him and embrace Him. He wants us to be able to come boldly before the throne of grace in the name of His Son. He was looking forward to the time when people would respond in worship to the Spirit of truth revealing aspects of His character. Worship is a response of love to God. We love because He first loved us, and the revelation of the unending flow of His delight in us provokes an unending flow of worship.

Scripture compares God's love for us to a river. "They

drink their fill of the abundance of Your house; and You give them to drink of the river of Your delights" (Ps. 36:8, NAS). This river doesn't stop. It is meant to be fully received and freely given. It is a love relationship and is expressed in lover's talk:

> [The Bridegroom-King]...
> Arise My dearest darling
> And let us run to the higher place.
> For now is the time to arise
> And come away with Me!
> For you are My dove,
> Hidden in the split open Rock.
> It was I who took you—
> And hid you up high
> In the secret stairway of the sky.
> Let Me see your radiant face
> And hear your sweet voice.
> How beautiful your eyes of worship,
> How sweet and enchanting
> Your voice in prayer,
> For you are ravishing to Me!
> —SONG OF SOLOMON 2:13–14, TPT

Do you hear the passion of God's love in these verses? These are words of intimacy—a love poem for a bridegroom and bride, but also a picture of God's love for you and an invitation for you to draw closer and know Him more fully. As you come away with Him in quiet, secret times of worship, you receive His love and are filled with passion for Him.

NOT AN EVENT
BUT A WAY OF LIFE

So many people get a taste of God's presence, either in their own quiet time with Him or in a worship service, and think that's what it means to have an encounter with God's love. That's a good start, but our intimacy with Him is meant to be so much more. God actually wants to give you such an overwhelming revelation of His heart toward you that your eyes are filled with His glory—that you would be perfectly content never leaving His presence again.

God recently gave me a vision of a big, beautiful tent. People came to this tent and received magnificent gifts from God and were amazed by how awesome this event was. But I could hear a challenge in the midst of this event for it to be more than that. God wanted people who in their hearts would say, "I'm not even going back out. I'm going to live here in His presence."

God gives us that choice. We can have the presence of God as an event that happens every now and then, perhaps even every day during our yummy Daddy time with Him. Or we can abandon all and just go with Him. And that's what He wants—not to be an event in our lives but to be our continuous covering. When He says His banner over us is love, He means all the time. He wants us to be continually aware of His presence.

Years ago I was in a worship service when God spoke to me about this. I realized that churches talk about hosting God's presence with an attitude that says, "We're going to have a worship service at this particular time," and then we gather together and invite God in. He comes in and touches people, and it's beautiful. But God spoke to me that day and said, "Katherine, I don't want to be hosted. I want to host you."

Do you see the difference? If I host people in my home, I set an appointed time and they come over. Perhaps we have morning tea, and I go to my cupboard and bring out whatever I have to serve them. But I'm in charge because it's my house and they are the invited guests. I'm in control of the visit. And that's what we do at our churches and, in many ways, in our own time with the Lord. We invite Him in but maintain control of the visit. We set an hour for this and ten minutes for that, and we'll have a lovely time. And the Lord very often meets us on those terms.

But He would prefer to be the host. He wants a whole new mentality, a new wineskin for living in our presence. He says, "I don't want you to have Me come as an event in your life, or even again and again as many events. I want you to live in My presence." This is what it means to abide in Him. In Him we live and move and have our being.

~ ⌇ ⚘ ~

Worship isn't a demand; it's an invitation into intimacy. It's lovers' talk.

~ ⌇ ⚘ ~

When we live in His presence like that, we come together with others in worship and overflow with the glory of the presence of God. The fire and light of God are magnified in our fellowship. We begin to encourage one another with what the Holy Spirit is saying from His heart. And others come and feast with us because we have so much to give.

God rejoices every time you make an effort to come

to Him. He celebrates every step you take that moves you deeper into His presence. And He wants to open the eyes of your understanding more and more, as Paul prayed in Ephesians 1, until you know you are beautiful in His sight and you begin to recognize your glorious inheritance. You are redeemed and have been seated with Him in heavenly places, and now He wants to go with you and glorify Himself in you, doing exceedingly abundantly beyond all that you hope or can even imagine. This isn't the Old Testament pattern of beholding God and then going and doing stuff for Him, and then coming back and repeating the process. It's a new wineskin in which you behold Him continuously and live there in His presence. Then, in Him, you live and move and produce much fruit, as He promised.

LOVERS' TALK

God loves worship that comes not out of a spiritual obligation but out of a genuine heart response to who He is. The Holy Spirit wants to reveal more and more of the Father's love so we will fall deeper and deeper in love with Him. That was the motivation behind Paul's prayer in Ephesians 1—that we would receive a spirit of wisdom and revelation that enables us to know God intimately and have the eyes of our hearts enlightened so we would know the hope of His calling, the riches of our inheritance, and the greatness of His power toward those who believe. That is such a glorious prayer, and it's for those who are already believers as well as for all who will one day believe. God wants us to get revelation from the Holy Spirit about the deep, secret things of His heart.

Many Christians miss the point of worship, and as

a result, their time alone with God isn't as fruitful as it could be. God doesn't say, "Worship Me!", because His ego needs attention. Worship isn't a demand; it's an invitation into intimacy. It's lovers' talk. Every day He wants to reveal more of Himself to you so your heart will continually, unendingly respond to Him in love. Worship is hearing Him say, "You're the apple of my eye," and saying back to Him, "Oh, Lord, You're amazing!" It's beautiful.

Every person is made for this kind of intimate relationship with Jesus. Not everyone will respond the same way to Him, but everyone is meant to respond. He wants a true expression from your heart, an expression that comes in the form He created you to give. Some people, like my husband, aren't outwardly exuberant. Some, like me, will dance and jump up and down with excitement. God doesn't want your response of worship to be contrived or conditioned to look like someone else's or to fit in with society's expectations. He wants a genuine expression of your heart so He can be glorified in your personality.

That's why He invites you to come into a place where you are united with Him in glory—where you can live and be filled with the confidence of knowing that you're loved. He wants you to give yourself to Him without fear of what anyone else thinks. I've found that when I simply trust Him and let myself drown in His presence, the favor of God just swirls around me. It's extraordinary. And if you'll let yourself drown in His presence—if you'll make your "yummy Daddy time" your highest priority—you'll find yourself surrounded with His favor and His love.

Chapter 6

RESTING IN THE LORD

Miracles and the Chair in the Air

I WENT TO SLEEP a little worried one night. The Lord had promised that He would open doors in England for me to preach. I had been given many prophetic words over the years, and I had held the promise strongly in my heart. God had recently begun to stir it up in me, and it had become more intense. So in faith I had penciled England into my calendar, even though my calendar had become very busy. But as the time grew closer and there were no invitations to England—I didn't even know anyone there— I began to wonder. And to worry. And to consider other invitations for that time.

So on this night when I went to bed preoccupied with England, I had a dream. I was sitting in a chair in this dream, and the chair was suspended high in the air. I thought, "Wow, these are great seats!" Other people were there too, and we were getting ready to watch something great unfold before our eyes. But after a while I began to worry about how this chair was being suspended in air without a balcony or anything else to hold it up. I started to try to figure out how to stay in the chair without falling. Worry turned into panic, and I began to struggle to stay where God had already put me. And as soon as I began to struggle, the chair began to wobble. Then I woke up.

"That was weird," I thought. "Lord, were You trying to speak to me?" I believe it's wise to take everything to the One who is smarter than us—the revealer of mysteries, the Holy Spirit—so I asked Him. He began to speak to me and reveal that everything He has done for me and in me is not of my own making. "Do you think any of your effort has brought you to where I've placed you?" He asked. "Do you think your worrying and striving has brought about any of the miracles I've been doing? That all those invitations to do the things you love to do have come through your own efforts?" Of course not. I'm not causing myself to sit in heavenly places with Him. I'm seated with Christ in heaven because of His grace. He is upholding me supernaturally with His right hand, and all I have to do is sit back and trust Him. I don't have to fuss and fight, and I don't have to figure out how to maintain my position. I simply need to rest in it.

> We simply need to trust God and
> realize the things He put in us to do were
> really His idea in the first place.

The next day my assistant came in and was looking at my calendar. She asked me about the space I had left for England, and I told her I was just trusting God. She began to pray and declare the doors to England were open. That night I received an e-mail from a pastor in northern England who had just watched some of our YouTube videos at the prompting of one of his church members. His church—a Baptist church that was hungering for more of the Spirit—was about six miles from where Smith Wigglesworth lived, and they wanted to see a release of that anointing in their area again. He promised to gather some other churches together if I would come and minister to them.

"Well, I happen to have a week free," I answered, telling him the dates I had set aside. "Would that week suit you?"

"That's perfect!" he answered. God is such a good organizer. Hallelujah!

I had to repent of all my fussing. Jesus is seated at the right hand of the Father, the most privileged position in heaven. The revelation of this amazing truth washed over me as I meditated on it. I wondered why I fuss so much when all we really have to do is sit in the chair. We simply need to trust God and realize the things He put in us to do were really His idea in the first place. Who are we to try to make anything happen? I'm not saying we have no responsibility to act, but we're not to act in order to achieve a position. We act out of the position we've already been placed in.

Since then I have ministered in many parts of Britain, and at the time of this writing I'm on a plane on my way home from one of those ministry trips. I have just been preaching in eight-hundred-year-old Anglican cathedrals, and in just two weekends I have seen around sixty people come to Christ. The testimonies delight my heart as they come in, and I give God all the glory for teaching me to rest in the chair!

SWEAT LESS
AND LAUGH MORE

We have been seated with Christ in heavenly places. Whenever I start striving in my own strength, I have to remind myself to settle back into the chair and rest. Then I can release the riches of His glorious inheritance. It's just that easy. Amazing miracles begin to happen and incredible opportunities come, and all I'm doing is sitting in the chair saying, "This is great, God!" It's absolutely stunning to me.

Sometimes I'm reminded of my privileged seat when I minister to the sick. Recently in Georgia I was praying what I thought were my best prayers for the healing of a man who had come for ministry. I was working up a sweat as I was praying, and I could feel the anointing bouncing around me. But I just wasn't seeing the breakthrough this person needed. Then I felt the Holy Spirit remind me to rest back into Him. As I saw myself leaning back in the chair, the man was immediately healed. The next woman who came forward was struck down by the Holy Spirit and healed before I could even lay hands on her. Now people are often reporting that they are healed minutes before the word of knowledge is given. Resting in Him, I sweat less and giggle more with delight at seeing Him show up and show off. I am on a glorious learning curve as I discover that in Him I live and move and have my being.

A couple years ago a man named Gavin was brought to our meeting very ill with a rare form of non-Hodgkin's lymphoma. They said it was stage 4B cancer, meaning it was in the final stage and in multiple places in his body. His spleen had been removed, and the doctors had given him two weeks to live. Gavin was a young father with two young children, and he and his friends and family were desperate to see him healed, so they had churches all over the district praying for him. During one of his many hospital stays, he met a man in an elevator who was dressed in a suit and didn't speak to him. The man simply handed him a card that said "expect a miracle" before stepping out of the elevator and disappearing. Gavin never saw him again. There was nothing on the other side of the card—no name, number, or address, only those three words. Gavin held on to the card and put his hope in God.

The night he came to the Glory Gathering, Gavin was very weak, so we prayed for him in the middle of the meeting. I felt the joy of the Lord as I became aware of God and the greatness of His power overshadowing us. God wants to touch and heal people far more than we do; He just gets joy from involving us as we lean into Him. Gavin's knees buckled under the power of the Holy Spirit, and he said he felt a hand go into his stomach and pull the cancer out. The next day he was back in the hospital having tests, and the results astounded the specialists. There had been a radical shift in his condition, and the doctors couldn't understand what had happened. Today Gavin is alive and well.

Romans 8:1 tells us that there is no condemnation for those who are *in* Christ Jesus. We saw earlier that this word "in" in Greek is *en*, which conveys the meaning "positioned at rest." There is no condemnation for us when, by faith, we rest in the place that the Father has given us by His grace. Through the sacrifice of Jesus we can rest in Him on His throne at the right hand of the Father. We are seated in heavenly places with Him, and we need to allow this reality to become more real than our circumstances and situations. It is in Him that His power and glory are seen. Miracles just start to increase and increase.

I'm learning that it's very smart to just sit in the chair. It's glorious fun. It's as Maria Woodworth-Etter once said: "Stop begging, and get joy in your heart; then you will get something."[1] Sometimes the flesh will try to tell you, "You know, you should be worrying about this situation. What about that promise God gave you; it hasn't happened yet. What are you going to do about that?" I've learned to choose to sit in the chair. I'm not going to fuss and fight, and I'm not going worry about what hasn't happened yet or try to work it out.

There is no condemnation for me, there is no guilt that can burden my heart and tell me I'm not qualified to receive the promise God has given me. His perfect love casts out all fear—the fear that we haven't done enough to earn His favor, that we don't measure up to His standards, that He loves us only because He has to but not because He really wants to. We are the apple of His eye. If we believe in what He has done for us—that His death on the cross has already paid for every sin we have ever committed and every sin we will ever commit—we are qualified to receive every promise He has given.

POSITIONED AT REST

The same Greek word *en* is found in Philippians 4:13—"I can do all things through [*en*] Christ who strengthens me." Self-control, one of the fruit of the Spirit listed in Galatians 5, is derived from two Greek words, *en* (positioned at rest) and *kratos*, meaning power, might, dominion, and strength.

Because of our position of resting in Him, we have power and dominion over our appetites. So I can do all things when I am positioned at rest in the chair. Knowing that we have been given a new identity and that we now have the spiritual DNA and character of Christ, we're called to search out the privileges and power that come with our position.

If we believe in what He has done for us, we are qualified to receive every promise He has given.

This is the inheritance of everyone who truly believes. The great power that flows from God's throne will flow through you as you allow the truth of this privilege to unlock your faith. I have seen God step through me and touch people with stunning miracles, and you can see Him doing the same things through you as you learn to position yourself in faith at rest in the chair.

A baby who had heart problems was brought to us when I was leading a series of meetings in Georgia with one of our Glory City Church pastors. Having heard some of the testimonies from our meetings, his parents had brought him hoping for an encounter with God's healing power. We prayed for the baby, and the parents said when he was taken back to the doctor a couple of days later, his heart condition had vastly improved. Many other wonderful miracles happened in that meeting—some of the testimonies are on our Glory Gathering YouTube channel.

One of the most touching stories that weekend was that of a woman who had come to the meetings under protest. She had been an alcoholic who would often go on drinking binges that would last for weeks. She would wake up to drink, throw up the first beer, and then just keep drinking. She also had many health issues.

At the first meeting I received a word of knowledge about someone's leg, and the people this woman came with encouraged her to put her hand up, because they knew she had problems with her leg. After we prayed, she started walking around at the back of the meeting room. When we opened the altar for people to receive prayer, she came forward saying something had happened. There was mysteriously no pain left in her leg. She asked if I could pray for her eyes because she had been wearing both glasses and contact lenses as a kind of home remedy for her badly failing eyesight.

The next night she returned to the meetings absolutely beaming. She was walking without pain and was not wearing glasses. She got up to testify with her son that she now had no need of either her glasses or her contacts. That night she received Christ as her Savior. I later received a beautiful letter from her telling me her story and testifying that she had also been gloriously delivered from alcoholism and had gone on to be baptized in water and filled with the Holy Spirit.

Many wonderful miracles took place that weekend with many people testifying to being healed. Kaydence, an eighteen-month-old foster child, had suffered neurological damage when she was very young. Her eyes rolled around in her head without control, one wandering one way and the other another way. As a result, she had never walked because she had no sense of balance. Her foster parents brought her forward for prayer. People gathered around to watch as we commanded her eyes to straighten up, and in front of us all, her eyes straightened. One onlooker said he'd previously had grave doubts about the reality of God and His healing power, but when he saw that baby's eyes come together and begin to focus correctly, he gave his life to Christ on the spot.

I called the pastor, Tony Thompson, a couple of days after the meeting just to make sure the healing had "stuck." I didn't want to be testifying about it if Kaydence wasn't really healed. Tony gently chided me. "Pastor Katherine! Not only are her eyes straight, but she has started walking!" Christ in us is more amazing and glorious that I have ever dared to imagine, and resting in Him is more glorious than I ever dared to hope. In Him we live and move and truly have our being.[2]

Recently in South Carolina we heard a testimony that particularly blessed me. April was one of many who came forward to receive the baptism in the Holy Spirit and had been gloriously touched by God. I had prayed for her and then moved on to pray for other people when I noticed she was walking gingerly around the building, crying as she walked. I found out later that April had been in a convoy accident in Iraq when she was in the army. A land mine had exploded, her truck was sandwiched between two other trucks, and the bones in her foot had been smashed. She was flown out in a soft cast, but the bones in her foot failed to set properly, leaving her with terrible pain when she walked.

After further operations April was faced with having to wear big metal braces on her legs to ease the pain of walking. I don't even remember praying for her healing that night at the altar, but as the power of the Holy Spirit came upon her and baptized her, April felt God touching her feet. She removed her braces very carefully and began to test out her legs. She was weeping with amazement at the miracle that had occurred and came back for the next meeting to show us her healing. She came wearing normal shoes and carrying her braces. She was so excited that she could jump and bend and twist her feet with a full range of movement without any pain. She was also happy that now she could paint her toenails and wear pretty shoes![3]

One of the most unusual displays of power I have seen was when a man came forward for prayer one morning at a church in which I was ministering. As I reached out to lay hands on him, the power of God hit him and he flew backward—and the sole of his new shoe blew off! He had been having trouble with his foot and was instantly healed as the Holy Spirit touched him. He had to tape the sole of his shoe back on so that he could drive the church bus after the service.

At times the Holy Spirit will allow me to see into people's bodies and know what is wrong. I remember looking at a woman in one of the meetings and seeing fluid on her lung. I asked her if this was right, and she said yes and God instantly touched her. Other times the Lord will give me words of knowledge, and people will respond by saying that they felt something like electricity hit them and had been healed minutes before the word was given. Instead of responding to the word of knowledge by coming forward for prayer, more and more people are coming to say they had that condition a few minutes earlier but had already been healed.

At other times I've gone to pray for people and have been taken into what must be a trance. I remember this happening for the first time in a meeting when a couple came forward to ask me to pray for their son who was in a serious condition in the hospital. As I went to pray for them, I suddenly saw myself walk into his hospital room and lay my hands on him. The next day we heard that during the night the man had recovered and had been discharged that morning.

THE REST OF FAITH

These are the kinds of stories that will become commonplace if we learn to rest in our position in Christ. We don't need to figure out how to stay in the chair; it's supernaturally suspended by God's hand, and striving to maintain our position in it will only cause us to wobble. He does glorious things through us not because we have struggled to make them happen but because He's good.

So many Christians struggle to arrive at or maintain their position in Christ, never realizing that it doesn't come by struggling. It comes by resting in what He has already done. Think about when you're trying really hard to forgive someone who has offended you, for example. Have you ever been in that situation where you tell yourself again and again that forgiveness is a choice and that you are choosing to forgive? But then you see the person again, and all of those bitter feelings come up again. Even if you've been healed of the hurt of that offense, you feel condemned because you still have unforgiveness in your heart, so you try again to make that choice to forgive.

It's a losing battle, isn't it? But when you're fully positioned with Jesus by faith and resting in Him, you don't have to try to conjure up forgiveness in your heart. You can release the forgiveness Jesus already has. He has already paid for that person's sin. He says, "I've already forgiven them, and you no longer live; I live in you. So just rest in the forgiveness I've already offered and release that to the person who offended you." It's wonderfully liberating.

We need to stop striving forward and learn how to lean back.

The same applies to our righteousness. We struggle and strive to be righteous—to walk in purity and be holy as God is holy, as the Word tells us. But it also tells us to consider ourselves dead to sin and alive to God. It's already done. We don't have to crucify ourselves; we are already crucified with Christ. It's no longer we who live but Christ who lives in us. If we really believe that, then the key is to rest in the life He is living through us, not strive to live it ourselves.

This is how it works with anything in our Christian life. We don't have to conjure up some power within ourselves to heal the sick. Jesus never said, "If you are holy and committed enough, and if you figure out the right words to pray, then I will heal the sick through you." No, He says, "Just sit in the chair and release what was done. By My stripes, they are healed (Isa. 53:4–5). Now I give you the authority to release on earth what is already true in heaven." In heaven you are seated with Christ; you already have authority in that position, and you're a gate that releases healing, forgiveness, love, joy, and all the other blessings of God's kingdom.

Do you see how this works? We need to stop striving forward and learn how to lean back. I don't mean we are to be passive; we are responsible to take action as the Lord leads. But we perform the miraculous works of the kingdom from a position that has already been won for us and from authority we've already been given. And that's an enormously important difference.

This is how we do the works of faith. It's all from a position of resting in Him. It's from sitting in a chair supernaturally suspended above, and no worry or fuss or struggling can keep us there. In fact, that's what gets our focus off of our position in Christ and onto ourselves. When we enter into the truth of the finished work of the cross—that everything has already been done by the death and resurrection of Jesus—we can step into the works He has called us to do. And we can begin to release the love and the power of heaven on earth.

Chapter 7

BUILDING ON THE ROCK

The Foundation That Doesn't Move

PASTORS HEAR A lot of stories. We get an up-close view of people's struggles—the trials they are going through; the difficulties they face in their relationships, health, and finances; and the questions they have about God's involvement in their lives. I was recently flying home from a speaking engagement, where I had been hearing a lot of these stories from people going through hard times and getting very discouraged about their problems. After hearing so many negative reports, with no end to the difficulties in sight, I started to get discouraged too. I began to ask, "Lord, why? These are people who love You and serve You, yet bad stuff is happening to them. I don't get it."

I realized then just how tempting it is to draw inaccurate conclusions about God when you look too long at circumstances. If we're not careful, we can start to try to explain things in our heads and get a perception of God that isn't based on the truth of who He is but on our circumstances.

False perceptions of God easily develop into false doctrines about Him. The church has done this many times throughout the centuries. Many doctrines have been created to explain why people don't always get healed when they pray or why trials come into our lives. Although these explanations may make people feel better for a time, they actually dilute and change the gospel in many ways. The Bible says that if we start building our "truth" on experiences and circumstances, it's like building a house on sand.

There was a time in my life when I momentarily gave in to that temptation, and the Lord had to pull me back out of it. It was during my thirtieth year—the time when God had promised He would open doors for me to go into full-time ministry. For most of the year it seemed to be the worst year I'd ever had. I had started praying for the sick, including two very close friends of mine who had cancer—the friends I mentioned earlier in chapter 4. Both died. I was very discouraged, and that's when I made a conscious decision one night during worship. I told God, "I think it would be better if I don't mess with this whole healing thing. If I tell people You heal and then You don't, they might not think well of You. I really don't like the risk factor there. Maybe I should just stick with the prophetic thing."

A powerless gospel was
never Christ's intention.

That seemed very rational to me. Whole denominations have thought the very same thing, classifying healing as "too hard" and playing it safe to avoid the risks. It seems easier that way. When you lower your expectations, you don't have those embarrassing moments when explanations fail and you don't know what to say. You can chalk it all up to the mystery of God and focus on "safer" areas of ministry.

But God is shaking things and bringing us back to the truth of who He really is. His Word is emphatic about the miraculous, and we can't compromise its truth. Jesus said, "Heal the sick, cleanse the lepers, raise the dead, cast out demons. Freely you have received, freely give" (Matt. 10:8). A powerless gospel was never Christ's intention. He expected us to do greater works!

I love a statement made by California pastor Bill Johnson: "I will never lower my doctrine to my level of experience." That doesn't just apply to healing; it also applies to anything else God promises. A lot of the doctrines and beliefs we develop to explain God's ways and make theology safer don't have any basis in the Gospels. Only Jesus can be the cornerstone of our theology. He's the only foundation. He is perfect theology. Jesus always manifested Himself as the answer to anyone who came to Him for help. The same yesterday, today, and forever, Jesus is still the answer. And He is the rock, the chief cornerstone that we build on. I am reminded of something Smith Wigglesworth once said, "I am not moved by what I see. I am *moved only by what I believe*...no man looks at appearances if he believes. No man considers how he feels if he believes. The man who believes God has it."[1]

THE ROCK AND THE SAND

Many of us who went to Sunday school as children probably learned this catchy little song: "The Wise Man Built His House Upon the Rock." When the rains came down and floods came up, the house on the rock stood firm because its foundation was solid. That song comes from a very profound and sobering message Jesus shared with His followers about the difference between being wise and being foolish:

> Whoever comes to Me, and hears My sayings and does them, I will show you whom he is like: He is like a man building a house, who dug deep and laid the foundation on the rock. And when the flood arose, the stream beat vehemently against that house, and could not shake it, for it was founded on the rock. But he who heard and did nothing is like a man who built a house on the earth without a foundation, against which the stream beat vehemently; and immediately it fell. And the ruin of that house was great.
>
> —LUKE 6:47–49

Wisdom builds on the rock. If we even begin to think ourselves so clever and presumptuous that we can build on anything other than the gospel of Jesus, we'll end up very confused and brokenhearted. Paul said that no one can lay any other foundation than what has already been laid down in Jesus (1 Cor. 3:11). Anything else is unstable. Other foundations will lead us into fear and discouragement and despair.

Jesus is the way, the truth, and the life (John 14:6), and in His life there is righteousness, joy, and peace in the Holy Spirit (Rom. 14:17). He wants you to step into the fullness of His kingdom and then go and heal the sick and tell people that the kingdom of God has come upon them. You may be tempted to assume He's the God who's causing your issues, but He isn't. He's the God who has come to be the answer to your issues. Whatever your trial or challenge, God's desire is to turn it around for your good (Rom. 8:28).

I've had to learn to apply this truth to everything that tries to come across my mind. The answer is always Jesus. That's our foundation. Whatever the problem is, He's the answer—it's in Him somewhere. We try to become problem-solvers, but the real solution is to look to Jesus in everything. We have to take captive everything that exalts itself against His supremacy, every thought that doesn't acknowledge Him as the answer. We have to recognize that there is an enemy prowling around who wants to lead us into lies and to despair, but Jesus, who is the answer, wants to lead us into hope.

In John 9 the disciples start asking questions as to why the man they saw was born blind.

> As He passed by, He saw a man blind from birth. And His disciples asked Him, "Rabbi, who sinned, this man or his parents, that he would be born blind?" Jesus answered, "It was neither that this man sinned, nor his parents; but it was so that the works of God might be displayed in him."
>
> —JOHN 9:1–3, NAS

I love the Lord's response. He made it clear that it wasn't about who sinned: it was about God being glorified by being the answer. Instead of being caught up with the questions, just look to the One who is the answer.

This is why it's so important to be vigilant about our thoughts. We must never allow circumstances to drag us down into discouragement and despair. Rather, we must focus our thoughts and fix them on the only one who is truth. Discouragement will try to come into our minds to lower our heads, but Jesus wants us to lift our heads and make us radiant. He doesn't want us looking down; He wants us looking up. He is the answer to all the questions we might have, and if we look to Him, we have hope.

WHAT IS YOUR FOUNDATION?

Your actions and reactions will always flow from your foundation, whatever it happens to be. So the crucial question is this: What is your foundation?

Many people are living like King Saul's grandson Mephibosheth. After David became king of Israel, he asked if there was anyone left in the family of Saul to whom he could show favor. One of Saul's former servants mentioned Mephibosheth, a son of Jonathan, who had been David's best friend (2 Sam. 9). Mephibosheth was lame and living in Lo-Debar—a town whose name means "no pasture" or "no promise"—and was apparently living a life that fit the description. David called him from this unsatisfying, unfulfilling place and invited him to eat continuously at the king's table as one of the family. It's a great picture of what God does for us, but many believers aren't taking advantage of His generosity and are still living in unsatisfying places. God wants us feasting at the king's table. He doesn't want us to be basing our lives on false foundations and wrong conclusions. He wants us to live from the right foundation.

So it's vital to ask, "What do I believe? What foundation am I building on? What is the anchor of my soul?"

If I'm following Jesus, I'm not able to come to any conclusion about God's will in any issue other than, "This is who I know Him to be." I'm not reaching for a distant hope, wondering if it's God's will to heal or to save or to meet a desperate need. I already know that's who He is—the provider, healer, Savior, deliverer, and so much more—so that's the truth on which my thinking has to be built.

I believe He brings beauty for ashes, that He makes all things work together for the good of those who love Him and are called according to His purposes, that He hears the cries of those who call to Him, and that He is mighty to save. There are no "buts" about this. When I run into a discouraging situation, I don't have to figure things out; I just deliberately remember what I believe. I already know. I know the nature and character of Christ, and all my theology must be built on Him. He is the rock on which I stand.

Yes, He Is Willing

Once when Jesus was teaching and multitudes were following Him, a leper came and worshipped Him. "Lord, if You are willing, You can make me clean," the leper said. Jesus put His hand out immediately and touched the leper. "I am willing," He said. "Be cleansed." And immediately the man's leprosy went away (Matt. 8:1–3).

When I was on the plane thinking about the people who were discouraged from wrestling with huge issues in their lives, I thought about this and all the other stories in the Gospels when Jesus healed those who came to Him. I had to choose either not to get discouraged or to build a doctrine that claimed God can't be trusted to look after families and people with needs. I decided I would think about every time someone came to Jesus with pain or sickness or a messy situation.

⌒ᕙᕗ⌒

Faith isn't what I see with natural eyes; it's the hope of what is unseen.

ᕙᕗ

What did He do? Was there ever a time when He said, "Oh, that's too bad for you. But this is really better for you, so I think I'll leave you in this condition"? No, of course not. Every single time someone asked for His help, He gave it. He came through in every situation and did what was needed. He never turned someone away with an unmet need. He manifested Himself to them as the answer.

The Gospels make this clear, but if you start looking around at people who haven't been healed, you can easily slip into despair. I've had to come to the place where I just remember what I do believe. Jesus is the answer. Faith isn't what I see with natural eyes; it's the hope of what is unseen. If I look at people's problems for too long, I can really start to focus on the negatives. But if I look specifically at the positives, they really can far outweigh the negatives. That's why we can't base our doctrine on experiences, whether good or bad. We base it on the cornerstone of the gospel. And the gospel doesn't say, "You know, it's better if you stay sick." It says Jesus healed everyone who came to Him.

While I was grieving over my two friends who died of cancer, in that time when I tried to put this healing call away because it was too risky, I received an open vision during worship, and God told me I must believe. (Never discount what God wants to do through worship, by the way. It isn't a presentation or a performance; it's a platform for us to encounter God. He can speak a word during worship that will set you free.) It was that simple and direct. Hearing God speak so clearly settled it for me.

I knew what God had said about laying hands on the sick and healing them. He said these signs would accompany those who believe. I had been receiving visions since I was twenty-three; often I was unable to get off the floor at home as I was groaning in birth pangs and having visions of fireballs going out into audiences and healing the sick as I preached all over the world. I had watched every video I could find about people with great healing ministries from previous generations. I had dug into this truth and given myself to feeding on the faithfulness of God.

This made me a nuisance in Bible college. I have a very passionate personality, and it got stirred up when the lecturers were trying to teach that God, in His sovereignty, doesn't always want to heal people—that sometimes there's a better way, something He wants to teach people in their sickness, and some mysterious way He's glorified in that. This teaching really bothered me because, at its core, it means that whenever I go to lay my hands on someone to be healed, I would have to ask myself if this person was one of those whom God didn't want to heal. How can you ever pray confidently in faith for anyone's healing if you believe that? To me that was like a red rag to a bull, and it provoked that kind of reaction in me.

So I prepared a fantastically brilliant message to convince them of the truth. I was given the opportunity to lead chapel, and I had decided I was going to deliver that message and correct their bad theology. But God woke me up in the middle of the night before that chapel service and wouldn't let me give that message. "Katherine, you don't love them enough," He told me. "I want you to talk about love."

"But God, they need to know this truth!" I said. That didn't sway Him. He wouldn't let me preach that message in the spirit that had provoked me to give it. I had to get up in chapel the next day and preach a sermon about how much God loves us. He protected me from doing what so many do today, which is get into very nasty arguments about theology. People can even get really mean about grace, and grace is supposed to be lovely! Yes, there are foundations we can't compromise, but we aren't supposed to get mean and knock people in the heads with our truth. The truth must be spoken, but it must always be spoken in love.

I was prepared to go to war with those lecturers over what God says about Himself, and He told me to drop it. I was ready to give them the truth, but not in love. God had to teach me some things about not being arrogant and puffed up with knowledge. He told me just to let it go.

Since that time we've seen so many people healed. We've seen more miracles than I can write down or even remember. We've seen spina bifida healed, people without eardrums being able to hear, crippled fingers straightening up and growing out, cataracts disappearing, people throwing away their canes and being able to walk; cancer, hepatitis C, and diabetes disappearing; and so much more. It's just extraordinary what God has done. It's enough to make me realize that, after all, He's actually smarter than I am! His thoughts and His ways are so much higher than mine.

THE TRUTH
ABOUT HEALING

I'll admit I got a bit stubborn about this at Bible college, but the experience drove me to look at healing in the Bible more closely. I had to know for sure what I was going to believe. I went searching for the truth about healing. I examined every single time in the Gospels when someone who was sick was brought to Jesus. This study confirmed what I mentioned earlier—that there isn't a single case of someone coming to Him for healing and being turned away. Not once did He say, "It would be better for you spiritually to remain sick." Yet we've built whole doctrines on this idea, and entire denominations have accepted them. That makes us feel better about our experience, which often seems to fall short, but it can't make us feel any better about what the Bible actually says. Too often there has been a gap between what it says and what we experience.

I believe one of the reasons for that gap is a prayer I hear all the time: "Lord, if You want to heal me..." The belief that healing often isn't God's will has the effect of undermining our faith. If we don't know and understand who Jesus is, we can't approach Him in faith and assurance. We can't pray in faith while we're also questioning whether He wants to heal, and James 1:6–7 says we don't receive anything from God if we doubt when we ask. Doubt completely undermines us. It's like shifting sand, and it makes our house fall. When our confidence begins to waver, that's when we have to go back to our rock, our foundation of truth, which is knowing the nature of God. In Jesus we see what He's like. We know it's His desire to heal because He healed everyone who came to Him.

There's a great illustration of this dynamic in the Gospels. The disciples were trying to heal a boy who was having seizures—he had epileptic fits and would sometimes roll into the fire—and they prayed without seeing any results (Matt. 17:14–21). They could have done what we do and come up with reasons God didn't want to heal, and perhaps they would have done just that if Jesus hadn't shown up on the scene. They could have devised all sorts of explanations about this boy or his parents having some hidden sin that was keeping him from being healed. They could have brought their beliefs down to their level of experience. But was it Jesus's will to heal? Yes! We know this because when He arrived, He healed.

It is still God's will to heal. Jesus came to give us life and life more abundantly (John 10:10). A lack of results is not an indication of His will. Jesus's response to the disciples was aimed at bringing their experience up to the level of His desire. He urged them to believe, assuring them that even faith the size of a mustard seed would be enough. He made it clear that they could do the works He was doing and that they would do even greater works because He was going to be with His Father.

Once when I was speaking about God's will for healing, I began to pray at the end of the session as I usually do. The first person I prayed for jumped up and said, "I'm healed, I'm healed!" Then a man took his hearing aids out because he had been healed. A man who had brought his Muslim wife for prayer was there, and even though there was terror in her eyes before I prayed for her, she was suddenly at peace afterward. She was not only delivered but also saved as we led her to Christ. A toddler who had hearing aids was asleep when I prayed for him—he didn't even know anything was going on—but the next morning when his mother tried to put his hearing aids in, he said, "No! Too loud!" It was a wonderfully joyful experience as God began to demonstrate His will to heal.

DON'T BE MOVED

This foundational truth about healing being the will of God, as well as all other foundational truths about God's true nature and His promises and purposes for us, are worthy of building our lives on. All of our theology has to come back to what we know about Jesus. If any thought, perception, or idea doesn't match up with the nature of Christ, then it isn't solid. It isn't true. Jesus is the truth.

I've found that when I start to get discouraged by what I see, it's usually because I'm trying to figure out what I was never called to figure out. There's a danger in that. We were never equipped to understand everything that happens or to answer every "why" anyone asks us. We are, however, equipped to trust God as the answer in every situation and stake our faith on who He is and what He has said.

Why do we get so off track on this? One reason is that we mentally react to circumstances and situations in our day-to-day lives, and we interact with futile thoughts and engage in internal discussions about "why."

Here's what happens: When you have given your heart to Christ, invited Him into your life, and received His mercy, you now have Him living on the inside of you. You have His hope, a strong foundation you can rest on. But that isn't the end of it. He wants all of you. He's a jealous God, and He wants you to enter into life more abundantly.

He says, "I have it for you—all the blessings and joy you ever need. Here they are. Come feast at My table!" And the enemy comes in and says, "Don't go over to that table just yet. Let's think about this."

We're supposed to be able to feast in Christ continually, not based on our circumstances but on the foundation of our hope. We're supposed to be cheerful because of the hope we have within us. But instead of feasting, too often we are waylaid by the enemy and his deceptions. We start to think about problems we weren't designed to solve, and we begin mentally interacting with issues and situations that get us tied up in knots. We spend an inordinate amount of time in mental conversation with these issues— and, in the process, lose our joy, our peace, and our trust.

If that describes you, ask the questions I ask myself in those situations: "What do I really believe? Why am I thinking about this so much?" If you're like me, the thoughts are probably based on some fear or anxiety. And when I remember what I really believe—that my foundation is based on who Jesus is—I realize I have no need to be afraid. I've listened to a lie. I'm following a detour of the enemy, and it leads me to a "feast" that doesn't taste very good. God says, "Build your life on the Lord Jesus Christ."

That's the rock we're to build on. God is going to come through. I don't have to worry about all that stuff I was worried about. I don't have to try to figure it out. I just have to believe because faith in Jesus is what my life is built on. Whatever the problem is, He's the answer. He's our peace, joy, hope, and love.

One of David's psalms expresses this attitude beautifully:

LORD, my heart is not haughty, nor my eyes
lofty. Neither do I concern myself with great
matters, nor with things too profound for me.
Surely I have calmed and quieted my soul, like
a weaned child with his mother; like a weaned
child is my soul within me. O Israel, hope in
the LORD from this time forth and forever.
—PSALM 131

The words of this psalm are like God saying, "I don't
want you to turn yourself inside out. I don't want you to
try to figure things out. I want you to look to Me in faith
and trust."

We see the opposite of this in the Book of Job. God
let Job and his friends go on and on about why all the
bad things were happening to Job. Job kept asking why,
and his friends had no shortage of answers. But those
answers were false foundations. When God was finally
invited into the discussion, He began to ask them questions that caused them to look at who He was. Instead of
answering the questions, God asked Job questions to get
him to see who God was. Only then did the situation get
resolved for Job.

God is not trying to get us looking deeper and deeper
into why things have or haven't happened the way we
wanted or expected. He keeps prompting us to look at
Jesus as the answer. Everything else is sinking sand.

The only weapon the enemy has against you is deception, so he's continually trying to waylay you and get you
to build your house on something else. But he can only
offer a house of cards on a shaky foundation. The solution
is to be fixed on God all the time.

That means we have to cast down every imagination

that exalts itself against the knowledge of Christ and take every thought captive (2 Cor. 10:3–5). In other words, anything that is not built on who Jesus is—anything that exalts itself above the foundation, anything that's trying to come in and get preeminence in our thinking—must be demolished. We shouldn't even entertain it because it's trying to steal from us the hope and joy God wants us to live in.

A lot of people don't know this, but God wants us to wake up happy, go to sleep content, and walk around fearlessly in between. His perfect love casts out fear, and He gives us the peace that passes understanding. When things are going wrong, we can have a special peace provided directly by His Spirit. There is a joy inexpressible and full of glory that's available to us all the time. He means for us to experience these things fully.

Another reason we get distracted from our true foundation is that we sometimes base our faith on the beliefs and practices of people around us. In his early days Mahatma Gandhi was drawn to Christianity. He read the Bible and went to a church, but the church wouldn't let him in because of his color. He decided he didn't want anything to do with Christianity.[2] That's a terrible tragedy, and we should pray that never happens again to anyone. But other Christians should never be anyone's basis for believing anyway. If we try to build our faith based on other people's beliefs or practices of Christianity, we would be settling for a terribly shaky foundation.

I've watched several great people of faith fall, and it's tragic when the people who followed them fall with them. It always makes me aware of how easy it is for human beings to base our beliefs on the wrong foundation. Pastors, teachers, apostles, and other leaders are all just under-shepherds of the one true shepherd. If some-thing happens to them, that's sad. But it doesn't change who the shepherd is. When the rains come and the floods rise, the houses built on the Rock still stand.

God wants us to wake up happy,
go to sleep content, and
walk around fearlessly in between.

One other reason we get distracted from our true foundation is not knowing how to approach Him in faith. Many people have said to me, "I don't experience God like you do. I don't know how to just lean back and rest in Him like that!" I tell them anyone can get a hug from God, and there are at least two simple ways to do that.

One way is to lean on, depend on, and rely on the Word of God. It's the truth. That's where our hope is unveiled. Knowing His truth as it is revealed in His Word can be your entrance into rest. Understanding how He feels about us allows His perfect love to flow into our hearts and acti-vates our faith.

But you can also allow Him to write on the screen of your sanctified imagination. As a creation of God Himself, made in His image, you have been given an imagination. Like a blank whiteboard, your imagination is neutral; what you allow on the screen is what is important. God can write on it, you can write on it, and the enemy can try to write on it, tempting you to entertain thoughts and fears. You have the choice as to what you entertain and what you reject. If a bad thought comes, it doesn't make you bad, but it must be rejected, not given room to expand. God also wants to write on that screen, your sanctified imagination, to help you lean on Him, to feel His embrace, or to receive whatever encouragement you need from Him.

There's a common objection to this idea: Can't we just imagine our own stuff? The answer is yes, we can. But these images don't have to be our own thoughts. We can ask the Holy Spirit to write on the screens of our imaginations. Scripture teaches us that if we ask God for something good, He isn't going to give us something bad. We can ask Him to show us things from His heart, and He delights to do it.

I've seen this happen plenty of times before. In the last chapter I mentioned a couple who wanted me to pray for their son who was in the hospital. It was a really bad situation. I began to pray for this young man, imagining him in the hospital. As I did, I went into a trance in the middle of the meeting. It began as my imagination, but it became so intense it went from being my imagination to a real encounter. I saw myself go into the hospital room, lay my hands on this man, and declare his healing.

The next morning the parents contacted the church to report that at that very moment when we prayed, something happened. Their son was going to be discharged from the hospital the following day. Was that "just my imagination"? No, the Holy Spirit took the screen of my mind as I offered it to Him and led me where He wanted to go. That's not at all a New Age deception, as some people think. God gave us our imaginations, and we have every right to use it in partnership with His Spirit to envision the truth He has told us. So when we receive comfort and encouragement from Him—and long, big hugs—on that screen, we're only experiencing what He has said is true.

Anyone can do this. Try it in worship sometime. Imagine yourself receiving a big hug from God. Ask the Holy Spirit to help you. He may lead you into a vision— that's where most visions are written and displayed, after all—or He may just let you enjoy the images He is gently impressing on you. Either way you can be confident that if you've asked Him for something good, He isn't going to give you something bad. He'll give you truth, not deception. All the blessings and gifts of the Spirit are available to those who ask and believe.

In order to stay fixed on our foundation, we quit trying to figure everything out, we look to Jesus and not other people as the answer, and we lean on God and rest in Him. It doesn't always feel like we're standing firm on the rock when we do that, but we are. Anchoring ourselves in what we really believe—in the character and nature of Jesus—is a vital key to walking in the miraculous and living from the right foundation.

When I was in England recently, someone gave me a crocheted lace decoration that was wrapped around a rock. It was a prophetic picture of me, they said—delicate and fragile on the outside but built on the rock. I thought that was a beautiful, tangible picture of what all of us are like. We have God inside us, no matter how fragile or sensitive or weak we might feel. We are strong on the inside because we build on the foundation of Jesus in everything we do.

No Holding Back

Let's go back to the truth that our actions and reactions will always flow from our foundation. If that's true, then what's your foundation? And if you aren't sure you're really building on Jesus alone as your foundation, how can you know?

How do you feel about yourself? If it's anything other than really happy, you're building at least a little bit of your life on the wrong foundation. God wants to give you overflowing joy and peace that passes understanding. If you wake in the morning and try to gauge how you are by your feelings, that's a symptom of building on shifting sand. Wake up instead and declare, "This is the day that the Lord has made; I will rejoice and be glad in it!" God doesn't want us to waste our time with sand at all. If we're really going to walk in the miraculous, knowing our foundation is crucial. We have to build on the rock, insisting on the truth: "I'm a new creation in Christ. Old things have passed away. I've been made new. As He is, so am I in this world."

~~~

**Don't give up, and don't settle
for false explanations of
why things aren't happening yet.**

~~~

If you have any circumstances in your life that are trying to weigh you down and make you look at them instead of at Jesus, be like the psalmist and refuse to give yourself to those things. Don't concern yourself with matters you weren't designed to figure out; instead, calm and quiet your soul like a weaned child, and hope in the Lord alone. Go straight to God and let Him wrap His arms around you. In His light you'll see light. Jesus is the answer to everything you're going through and the key to living in miraculous power.

He's the one who says, "This is My will in every situation. I can work everything together for good. I can cause My power to flow through you to heal and deliver. Just trust Me, even when you don't feel like you can, and recognize that I am for you. I am not against you, and I'm not holding back. My power, My peace, and My love are available to any who will keep pressing in and believing in Me as the only foundation of their faith. If you will bring Me your questions, I will show you that I am the answer. I will glorify Myself in you because that is My nature. It's who I am."

Keep pursuing Him for the miraculous. Don't give up, and don't settle for false explanations of why things aren't happening yet. Measure everything by the standard of Jesus—His nature, His character, His ministry, and His words. He's the same yesterday, today, and forever.

Remember, this is a day of awakening. The gospel includes all kinds of miracles, including healing. God is opening our eyes to see in the light. He's not hiding His will and leaving us to walk around in the dark. He wants to enlighten our hearts in the knowledge and understanding of who He is. In every single circumstance, every single time, He provides the answer, never once withholding. True love gives. That's God's nature. The more we realize the truth of who He is, the more we are able to build on that foundation. And the more we will see His power manifesting in our lives.

Chapter 8

SOWING YOUR PAIN

The Promise of Double for Your Trouble

M Y MOM AND dad divorced when I was quite young, and because my father lived about twelve hours away, my younger brother and I were able to see him only a couple of times a year. My brother got himself into some trouble at school, so at the last minute one year my father decided to take him with his new family on their planned vacation to Fiji, traveling first class. Dad knew my brother needed some father time with him. I can understand that now as an adult, but as a teenager I felt a little rejected being left behind. It didn't seem fair. I had never been on an overseas trip and had certainly never been anywhere first class.

Years later I was invited along with several others to speak at a Hindu school in Fiji. The students were learning about religious festivals, and because Hinduism can accommodate many gods and diverse religious beliefs, we were to share about the meaning of Easter. The vice principal, a Christian, had her own purpose in inviting me; she had heard my testimony of having been abused and then marvelously healed by God. As I've shared, the Lord did a huge work in my life, setting me free from deep roots of rejection, abandonment, and shame. Many of the girls in this school had also been abused, and the vice principal was concerned about the high rate of suicide among the students. So she asked if I and the other pastors would give our testimonies during the three hours we were teaching about Easter.

The other pastors did a beautiful job of explaining how Jesus is the only way to salvation, and I gave my testimony of being supernaturally healed by God from deep emotional wounds. I told about my experience of seeing myself as a little girl with an ugly face, of how the ugliness floated away like a mask coming off, of how God stroked my hair, and then of my conversation with Him when He showed me myself as a woman of dignity in heaven. We gave an altar call at the end of the three hours, and 90 percent of the high school students and teachers gave their lives to Christ. The principal asked the local pastors to send the school some follow-up material on serving the one true God. It was an astonishing harvest.

I'll always remember how amazed some of the students were when they heard about having a relationship with God. "You have a God who actually speaks to you!" they marveled. They learned that it's possible to know God personally—that we don't worship an idol, an empty philosophy, or a religious system. We worship a God who cares so deeply for us that He knows the deepest wounds of our hearts, and He knows how to get in there and heal us the way no one else can do. When we cry out to Him, He can come in with a solution that meets our deepest needs. Being involved in introducing Him to nearly two hundred students was a glorious experience.

On the plane as I was traveling back home, still

rejoicing at what God had done, I heard Him speak to me. He said, "Double recompense, Katherine." I knew He was referring to a scriptural truth I had been learning— His promise to give us double for all the trouble we have been through. I immediately remembered that time years before when my father was traveling first class to Fiji and had chosen my brother rather than me to go with him. Now God was giving me what I missed then—and He was doing it in a way that brought glory to Him and built His kingdom. Even the little things I had forgotten about had not escaped His attention.

God just loves to take our pain,
our shame, and our hurt and
give us double for our trouble.

A couple of years later I was traveling by myself from Finland to minister in the United States, and I found myself upgraded to first class. As I sat up in the front of the plane being offered lobster and moose (yes, as in the big, hairy Finnish animal!), the Lord again whispered to me: "Double recompense." Not only had He healed my heart from the wounds of abuse and the sense of rejection, He was now allowing me to go around the world and give so many other souls the comfort He had given me. And He was sending me first class!

In fact, God continues to give "double recompense" for those wounds of the past, both large and small. I frequently have supernatural favor on airplanes now; I'm a magnet for it. Even airlines I rarely fly will upgrade me to first class for no apparent reason. I don't deserve it, of course. It isn't about that at all. God just loves to take our pain, our shame, and our hurt and give us double for our trouble. I have learned that, based on His promises, I can now take any pain, shame, or disgrace I have suffered and exchange it for His blessing. Not only will He restore us and heal us, but also He wants to do exceedingly, abundantly above all we can ask, hope, or imagine.

AN EXTRAVAGANT PROMISE

Isaiah 61 is a passage about restoration. The Israelites had gotten themselves in trouble and had been disciplined for it, but the prophecy in Isaiah demonstrates the heart of God for His people. Even though they had sinned, God promised double recompense for the trouble they were bringing on themselves. His plan was for restoration, for a double blessing. So the passage talks about giving them beauty in place of their ashes, the oil of joy in place of their mourning, and a garment of praise instead of their spirit of heaviness (Isa. 61:3). Then God promises this:

> Instead of your [former] shame you shall have twofold recompense; instead of dishonor and reproach [your people] shall rejoice in their portion. Therefore in their land they shall possess double [what they had forfeited]; everlasting joy shall be theirs.
>
> —ISAIAH 61:7, AMP

The passage goes on to explain how God, who loves justice, will give His people visible blessings and a reputation among the nations. He will clothe us with garments of salvation and cover us with a robe of righteousness, adorning us in the way a bride and groom adorn themselves for their wedding.

This is so important to understand because many people think that when they are going through hard times, perhaps God has withdrawn His favor. I used to let my thoughts go there, wondering if God was on my side. I would read marvelous promises, but many of them were only for "the righteous," and I wondered if I qualified.

Our past wounds have a way of crippling our faith and distorting our perceptions of God.

Sometimes I felt righteous because I had been doing well, and other times I didn't feel righteous at all. Was my righteousness enough to qualify me for the promises? Sometimes it certainly didn't seem so. But God tells us clearly that we have been justified in Christ—not by our works, but by believing in Him and trusting that what He did for us on the cross was enough. If we have faith in Jesus, we have been justified. And if we have been justified, the promises—including this one about double recompense— are for us.

What does this have to do with knowing God's love in order to walk in miracles? This is where many people get sidetracked, by doubting either God's love or His power in the midst of their pain. Our past wounds have a way of crippling our faith and distorting our perceptions of God. They make us forget He is on our side. So we simply have to understand God's love and power if we are to walk in any level of victory. God can turn any situation around and make it fruitful. His love, not our behavior, is the basis for our righteousness. We are qualified for the blessing of double recompense not because we deserve it but because of His great love that never fails us. If we have placed our faith in Him, He is on our side.

THE PROMISES ARE YOURS

We know God is on our side because Scripture tells us He is. Paul made this absolutely clear in his letter to the Romans, which I'm quoting from the Amplified Bible so you can savor every word of its wonderful truths:

> We are assured and know that [God being a partner in their labor] all things work together and are [fitting into a plan] for good to and for those who love God and are called according to [His] design and purpose. For those whom He foreknew [of whom He was aware and loved beforehand], He also destined from the beginning [foreordaining them] to be molded into the image of His Son [and share inwardly His likeness], that He might become the firstborn among many brethren. And those whom He thus foreordained, He also called; and those whom He called, He also justified (acquitted, made righteous, putting them into right standing with Himself). And those whom He justified, He also glorified [raising them to a heavenly dignity and condition or state of being]. What then shall we say to [all] this? If God is for us, who [can be] against us? [Who can be

our foe, if God is on our side?] He who did not
withhold or spare [even] His own Son but gave
Him up for us all, will He not also with Him
freely and graciously give us all [other] things?
—ROMANS 8:28–32, AMP

It's easy for most Christians to believe these verses
about someone else. We put a lot of faith in God's love
for others. But these truths are about you. Paul is making
the point that if Jesus went to the trouble to die for you
and then rise again to give you new life, it would make no
sense for Him to withhold His best from you now. God has
already given the best that He has—His own Son. He has
cleansed us with Jesus's blood and forgiven us of our sins
so that we can have a deep, intimate relationship with Him.

He has put His own life within us by His Spirit, and
He has seated us at His own right hand. This is true for
everyone who has received Jesus as his Savior. So if you
have placed your faith in Him, you are justified already.
The promises are yours. You don't earn them or have to
grow into them. You receive them because God is good
and because He loves you.

God isn't on your side only if you've done well this week.
He isn't on your side only if you've prayed three hours
every day. He isn't on your side only if you've reached your
quota for good works recently. None of those things can
qualify you for His favor. He is on your side if you've humbled yourself and said, "I can't achieve holiness. I need your
righteousness, Lord." When Scripture says "if God is for
us," you don't have to stumble over the word *if*. You haven't
forfeited His favor by not being righteous enough; His
promises were never based on your righteousness anyway.

They are based on the righteousness of Jesus, and He has given His righteousness to all who believe.

So when you are going through a difficult time—trials, hardships, persecutions, or whatever else—you can still rest in the love of God and trust that all things are working together for your good. This isn't God just making the best of a bad situation; it's about His ability to completely turn it around and use it as a platform for miracles in your life. Regardless of whatever defeats you think you've suffered, they can actually become the source of resounding victories. So you can truly rejoice when you are persecuted or suffer any pain, shame, or disgrace. The Lord wants to give you double for your trouble.

The beautiful thing is that He doesn't do it because you deserve it but because His idea of justice is to give grace to the undeserving. The promise of beauty for ashes and joy in place of mourning was given to people who had brought the trouble on themselves. God invites us to bring Him our ashes and exchange them in faith for His beauty. It doesn't matter what comes against you; if God is for you, nothing can successfully come against you.

SOWING PAIN, REAPING JOY

My husband and I went through a season when someone really took a severe disliking to us and tried to cause us as much trouble as possible. This person threatened to get the media to publish negative stories about us, wrote to all the pastors we knew around the world, called Tom's job, and even threatened to stir up trouble with the Finnish embassy, for which Tom serves as an honorary consul. I just wanted it to stop and wondered why God wouldn't put an end to it. But Tom, in his wisdom, counseled me not to get drawn into reacting and reminded me to let it go and "sow" the pain as seed into the soil of what God is doing in our lives.

We endured each of these threats and rejoiced that God was working it all for our good. We have both learned that these kinds of things are God's battle to fight, not ours, and we can trust Him to give us double recompense for all the pain, shame, disgrace, dishonor, and injustice we experience. That very same year, not only did the media *not* publish any bad stories about us, but also they printed two good reports; my ministry invitations tripled; and the Finnish embassy gave Tom a knighthood!

The promise of Isaiah 61:7 is that God gives us twofold recompense for our former shame, pain, and disgrace. I've had to learn to trust this truth whenever people write terrible things on the Internet about me. Sometimes they see a YouTube video and feel the need to argue with it. Maybe they just want to be contrary, or perhaps they have an agenda against those who preach the things of the Spirit; maybe I just rub them the wrong way. I don't know, but we're told to expect opposition and even persecution if we are following God and speaking His truth.

The enemy hates God, and he hates each of us, so it's no surprise that he tries to discourage us. God wants to give us beauty for ashes, joy for mourning, and a praising heart instead of depression. He loves to see us revel with hope.

Now when people upload ugly YouTube videos or comments about me on the Internet, I sow the pain with joy and faith, claiming extraordinary favor on the Web. And we have it! Our channel is so effective in getting the gospel out that YouTube wants to pay us to advertise on our videos. When people reject me, I celebrate knowing that I can exchange that rejection for double favor to come. And you can approach all of your adversity in exactly the same way.

Whatever your pain, your faith in God's goodness will be rewarded and will bless the heart of your Father because faith pleases Him, and He delights to bless you more than you will ever know. He has a way of taking the pain we experience and turning it around so that we end up being blessed because of it. He bears fruit in our lives even through the worst things that happen to us. Adversity doesn't limit our capacity for the supernatural; it enhances it.

I've learned not to waste a drop of the pain. I take it up, sow it by faith, and say, "Double recompense, Lord." And what He does in response is wonderful. Now whenever I encounter trials, I actually celebrate. I don't enjoy them, of course, but I know the joy they are going to lead to. That's such a contrast from before. I used to play the part of a victim because I had so many issues and didn't know how to put them behind me. But when the Lord came to heal me, He came also to bring a revelation of restoration: that He not only wants to deliver us from pain, guilt, shame, and disgrace, but He also wants to restore double for our trouble. Now when I suffer from hardship or opposition, I put a claim in to heaven. I know it's going to work for my good. He replaces our ashes with beauty and our mourning with joy.

When the Lord spoke this promise into my life, I began to get militant with it. I would take my pain to God and thank Him that I could rejoice over what He would do with it. And whenever I sow my pain, I can expect a harvest. In every area people have tried to hurt us, we've been exceedingly blessed. I've seen it happen again and again.

Adversity doesn't limit our capacity for the supernatural; it enhances it.

Bad things sometimes happen. I think Scripture is clear about that, and so is our experience. We aren't immune from difficulties. Some people look at the hard things going on in your life and point a finger. "Well, something must be wrong," they say. "Obviously it isn't God's favor on you right now." But that's absolute rubbish, a religious lie from an old mind-set. We all go through things. But no matter what you're going through, even if it has been a long-standing problem, it's going to work together for your good.

The more pain it's causing you, the more delight you can have because the harvest is going to be really worthwhile. Whatever pain you might be in, whatever dishonor you've suffered, the Lord wants you to sow it by faith and believe that you are the righteousness of God and that you therefore have the right to claim the promise of double recompense. Put your faith in Him and take hold of His promise. Don't waste your pain. Sow it instead. Give it to God and know that He is faithful.

This is why Jesus could make such an amazing promise to His disciples. He told them that anyone who left land and homes, brothers and sisters, parents and children for His sake would receive one hundred times as much in this age and eternal life in the age to come (Mark 10:29–30). It's an extraordinary promise. No one who has given up anything for the sake of the gospel will fail to receive it back in this life.

Zechariah 9:12 echoes the promise of Isaiah and assures us He will restore double to us: "Return to the stronghold, you prisoners of hope. Even today I declare that I will restore double to you." Job went through incredible hardship but ended up having everything he lost restored to him twofold. God sees the whole story; He notices everything we have been through, and He will not stand back and withhold glorious, divine recompense for long. The blessings He gives will be greater than the losses we experience. We will receive at least double for our trouble, if not more.

BLESSED TO BE A BLESSING

When we experience pain, God doesn't just give us double recompense for our own sake. He multiplies our blessing by enabling us to bless others. This dynamic is expressed in 2 Corinthians 1:

> Blessed be the God and Father of our Lord Jesus Christ, the Father of mercies and God of all comfort, who comforts us in all our tribulation, that we may be able to comfort those who are in any trouble, with the comfort with which we ourselves are comforted by God.
>
> —2 CORINTHIANS 1:3–4

This is what I found when I shared my experiences with the students at the Hindu school. God healed me from all that pain in my past, which was an enormous blessing in itself. But the blessing didn't stop there. I was able to tell many other hurting students about God's compassion and His power to heal, and I enjoyed seeing them encounter Him for the first time. Whatever type of comfort He gives to us, we then get to go and give that same comfort to others. This is what double recompense is all about. Not only does He come in and heal the problem, but He also takes that healing and then uses it to flow out of us to encourage and comfort others.

So you can bring to God any pain you've experienced and exchange it for something wonderful. This is your inheritance, a promise He gives to all of His children who will take it by faith. It applies to anyone who is in Christ Jesus. A life of miracles isn't for those who have it all together; it's for those who have sown the seeds of their experiences by faith into God's kingdom. You can know beyond the shadow of a doubt that His faithful promises will be fulfilled in your life—and that the fulfillment will be a blessing to those around you.

In practical terms, here's how that works. When someone has done something nasty to me, or even just when the circumstances of life have been unkind, I take the pain, the disgrace, or the shame and sow it in faith, saying, "Lord, Your faithfulness is my shield and fortress to defend me. Your faithfulness surrounds me. You promised that You would give us beauty for ashes and joy for mourning, so here are my ashes. Here is my mourning. Here's my pain. I trust that there will be double honor for every disgrace, double restoration for every loss, double blessing for every pain."

You can bring to God any pain you've experienced
and exchange it for something wonderful.

Then I wait with joyful expectation to see what He does. All I have to do is sit in the chair—lean back, relax, and rest in His ability to fulfill His promises. When I haven't seen the circumstances work out yet, I am, as Zechariah 9:12 says, a "prisoner of hope." I hang on to what God has said and declare that He is going to keep His Word. I don't know how He will restore, but He will. I don't know how He will use the obstacles not only for my good but also for His glory, but He will, because I *know* Him. I don't know who else will benefit from the blessings He has given me, but someone will. Whatever comfort He has given me is also for me to give away.

This really is a remarkable truth. It means that there is nothing bad that can happen to us that can't also be turned around into a blessing for us and a benefit for God's kingdom. No matter how awful someone has been to us, no matter how terrible a disaster has seemed to us, it's never our job to fuss and worry about it. Our job is to sit back in the chair and sow all of the loss, knowing that we are prisoners of hope and God's faithfulness surrounds us like a shield. When we do that, the enemy is surely sorry he ever messed with us!

DON'T WASTE ANYTHING

I want to encourage you to wake up to the reality of where you are positioned today. You are in a place of regal authority, and you are allowed to lay hold of whatever Jesus has laid hold of on your behalf. He wants you to sit in the chair with Him and to know with a sense of majesty that you can declare His faithfulness over any circumstance you face.

When you know this, all of your pain and losses and shame can become the key to a double blessing. Don't waste any of it—not a thing. He can restore everything you ever lost. I know this from experience. He has given me more than double honor in places where I was dishonored. Some of the very people who have spoken against me have later asked me to come and work for them. It's amazing. God doesn't forget any of the details. If you will allow Him to watch over the promises and fulfill them in your life, if you'll allow Him to be Lord of every circumstance, He will reveal Himself in such a magnificent way that you will want to humbly bow and tell Him how amazing He is.

Remember that this isn't because we earn or deserve His recompense. It's because He loves us. His faithfulness surrounds us like a shield and invites us to rest in Him completely, as securely as a child rests in his father's arms. Only as we know the fullness of His love can we begin to enter into that rest. But if we can only grasp this—that His love compels Him to bless us and show us His favor even in our greatest pain and deepest wounds—we suddenly enter into fruitfulness as we've never experienced it before. He is so amazingly kind that He gives us double for our trouble—and He gives enough for us to share!

Chapter 9

DREAMING WITH GOD

When the Impossible Becomes Possible

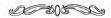

EARLIER I SHARED the story of how God called me to ministry at a time when that calling seemed impossible. He had spoken certain promises over me, and I had been dreaming about them. I saw fireballs going out over congregations, people getting up out of wheelchairs, miraculous healings taking place, and people getting saved. And I saw myself preaching on a platform, which really didn't seem likely for me as a woman or for the circumstances I was in at the time. But I realized that God had brought me to a place where He was inviting me to dream—to let the vision of His calling fill my heart and take my mind into daydreams about my destiny.

> We need to be people who are ready to say,
> "Lord, let it be to me according to Your word."

As I began to daydream, I would decree and declare God's faithfulness. "I *know* You are faithful, Lord," I would say again and again. "I *believe* You will fulfill Your promises to me. I don't understand it, and I can't see it in the natural realm, but I am choosing to trust what You are speaking to me. I will preach the gospel. I will lay hands on the sick, and they will recover. I declare that I will travel all around the world to preach the gospel and see people come to know You. You *will* confirm Your word."

I would walk around and say these things out loud. I'd write songs about God's promises. And even though it seemed like such a stretch to say these things and dream about them, I learned that this is what God wants from us. He doesn't want us to hold our visions as vague pictures and secret longings in our hearts. He wants us to hold them clearly before our eyes.

Many people are afraid to do this because they don't want to produce something out of their own imaginations. But as we've seen, our imagination isn't inherently bad; it's neutral. It's a blank screen waiting for someone to write on it. It can be written on by us, by the enemy, or by God. And many times that's how God speaks to us. He cultivates visions in our hearts and invites us to step into them. When we ask Him to fill us with His will for our lives, He may write it on the screen of our imagination. It isn't a one-dimensional screen but a fully interactive experience with Him. He wants us to see the dreams and step into them, walk around in them, speak them out, and say, "Lord, I believe."

When the angel came to Mary to tell her she would be the mother of Jesus, that's how she responded. She said, "Let it be to me according to your word" (Luke 1:38). In the following verses we are told that she believed, rejoiced, talked about the promise with Elizabeth, and later pondered all the testimonies about Jesus in her heart. She simply received what God was saying. We need to be people who do that, who take hold of what the Lord is saying and receive it by faith, who are ready to say, "Lord, let it be to me according to Your word." This is how God conceives His plans in our hearts. When we receive them and believe them and let our minds daydream about them, we begin to fly with Him wherever He wants to take us.

Whatever we focus on is what will develop in our lives.

God gives us a great illustration of this truth in Genesis 30. Jacob took fresh branches from certain trees and peeled off strips of bark, making white stripes on them. Whenever the stronger flocks of sheep and goats came to drink, he would put them in the water so they would conceive striped and speckled offspring. He and Laban had agreed that the spotted and streaked animals would belong to Jacob and the solid ones would belong to Laban. So over time all the stronger flocks began to be spotted and speckled, while the weaker ones remained solid colored. And this is how Jacob became prosperous. The animals conceived what was kept before their eyes.

That's how it works with us spiritually. Whatever we focus on is what will develop in our lives. What we keep before our eyes is what grows in our hearts. And the Lord wants us to put our focus on Him and the dreams He has for us. You can tell when you meet people who have been beholding their problems all day long. It shows. They are reflecting what they have seen with their own understanding. But if we behold God in His glory, we reflect Him. And if we behold the dreams He is writing for our lives, those dreams will begin to manifest. He wants us to consistently live in His presence so we can reflect His glory and let Him write on the blank screen of our hearts. Then we can dare to believe the great things He has planned for us.

Scripture tells us that as we delight ourselves in the Lord, He will give us the desires of our hearts (Ps. 37:4). As we enjoy the delight of His love and fellowship and fix our thoughts on Him, God will give us the desires that He wants to fulfill in our lives. If you're dreaming about laying hands on the sick and seeing them healed, if you're daydreaming about creative miracles, God has given you those desires. Learning to be led by what the Spirit of God inside is craving and longing is the door to real joy and satisfaction. What does your spirit long for? God has put deep longings in your heart, and you need to learn to listen to them.

WHAT DOES YOUR SPIRIT WANT?

One night I was preparing to sit down with the family and watch some TV with them. They were following a cooking competition, and I had very little interest in it, but I felt I should keep them company. I had spent all day with them, so it wasn't a matter of making up for lost time. I just felt that I should be with them. They don't watch a lot of TV, but as they are all cooking enthusiasts, it was something they really enjoyed.

As I walked toward the TV room, I felt the Holy Spirit tug on me and ask me what I really wanted to do. As I stopped and thought about it, I realized I was really crying out for some more alone time with God. My family wasn't going to feel neglected if I made a different choice this night. So I spent the next couple of hours fellowshipping with God in prayer and the Word and was blissfully happy. Sons and daughters of God are led by the Spirit of God, and His Spirit in us gives life and desire to our spirit. So ever since then I've been making a point of listening to the desire of my heart, the deep craving of my spirit.

God has created us to have life and life more abundant, but unless we allow Him to lead us, we can miss out on the fullness of joy He has for us. He knows all our needs and responsibilities and won't lead us to be irresponsible, but as we begin to yield to the One who is wiser than we are, He orchestrates our lives to be abundantly fruitful.

As you cultivate a life of love, you will begin to recognize that God loves for you to dream with Him. Whether they are big or little dreams, God wants to be leading you into a life of joyful adventure with Him. On my first trip to the United Kingdom, I had a day off to visit an old abbey. I walked through this Anglican cathedral and found myself moved with a burden and love for the Anglicans. I had gone to an Anglican girls' school, and my heart for the Anglican Church was stirred. I found myself telling a friend that I wanted to preach in Anglican cathedrals. Then I just began declaring out loud that I would be doing exactly that.

As it turns out, the brother of the Baptist minister who invited me to speak at his church in England came to the meetings I was leading, and within six months I had invitations to preach in some of these old stone cathedrals. In one weekend of speaking in three different Anglican churches, we had sixty people come into relationship with Christ. God had a dream for that, and He was just waiting for me to agree with it.

God even wants us to know that as we delight ourselves in Him, He cares about the little things. I experienced this clearly one night in Ohio on the first night of a conference at which I was speaking. One of the other guest speakers was sharing, and as the night grew late, I started thinking I would really love a cup of tea and maybe even a piece of cake to nibble on. I had just finished a series of meetings and was a little tired, and I could see the kitchen close by. I even toyed with the idea of slipping out to the kitchen to see if I could find some peppermint tea. As I was trying to decide whether or not that would be impolite, a woman came and set up a folding table beside me. (I was on the end of a row.) Then she brought out a tray with a china teapot of peppermint tea, a beautiful cup and saucer, and a piece of cake.

He enjoys doing life with you and leading you
into the dreams He has put in your heart.

Literally seconds after I had the thought, here was this woman presenting me with the very things I had just been thinking about. This wasn't a deep need, obviously, just something God enjoyed setting up for me. In fact, the Lord had prompted the woman earlier in the day, and she had arranged to have her best china brought from home just so she could surprise me and bless me that night. I had never even mentioned that I liked peppermint tea; she told me later that she knew Australians liked tea and just wanted to bless me. But I felt like God kissed me on the cheek with His over-the-top kindness that night. He does enjoy giving us the desires of our heart!

If He cares so much about little things, how much more does He care about you? God tells us to consider the birds and how well He takes care of them (Matt. 10:29–31; Luke 12:6–7); how much more will He take care of you? God wants to be with you as your Lord, Savior, friend, and lover, and He enjoys doing life with you and leading you into the dreams He has put in your heart.

Most of us already know God has a plan for our lives and dreams for us that He wants to be fulfilled. He says so clearly in Jeremiah 29:11: "'I know the plans I have for you,' declares the LORD, 'plans to prosper you and not to harm you, plans to give you hope and a future'" (NIV). But He wants us to know those dreams too. He wants to let us in on the plan, and then He wants to fulfill it for us. So if we will submit our imagination to Him, He will often speak to us through our daydreams, putting glorious thoughts and plans into our hearts.

AWAKENING THE DREAM

God is moving, and He wants us to move with Him. There is a glorious awakening going on, and He is inviting us to lean into it, to dive into the deeper things of His Spirit, and to follow Him into the fullness of our destiny. And when we learn to dream with Him, we will know how to move in sync with Him.

A friend recently asked me if I feel like I'm walking in a dream. She knew my story—how I had seen and declared that doors into nations would open, that miracles and healings would become common. I told her that this does feel like a dream. I'm walking in the things I used to dream about, and as I put them before my eyes, they eventually began to manifest. Why? Because they were God's dreams, and He had been writing them on my heart.

This is why experiencing the depth of God's love is so important. The more we have real intimacy with Him, the more He begins to impart His desires into us. And we can only have real intimacy if we are secure in His love—if we are free to trust Him and hear Him because we know how much He adores us. I can be really real with God and tell Him anything, but after I have asked Him to work out all of my stuff and take my issues into His hands, I then ask Him about His heart. That's when He reveals secrets, tells me what He wants me to do, and imparts His dreams into my life. And we have real intimacy in our relationship because there is honesty and depth there. When He becomes a holy addiction in our lives, we just can't get enough. And the more we become obsessed with Him, the more He reveals and entrusts Himself to us.

For a long time churches have taught us to climb ladders in the hope that we would one day be released into ministry. I've climbed many ladders and reached the top, only to find out they didn't take me where I wanted to be. All of them seemed to make false promises: "If you do this, then you will be able to do that..." and so on—a never-ending series of hoops to jump through in order to reach the goal and be rewarded. We need to be reminded who is actually the King of this kingdom. Is it men with their rules who tell us we need to earn the right to give away what's in heaven? That we have to prove ourselves before we can begin to release the blessing of God? No, of course not. We've lived under a lie that takes the grace of God and makes us climb stairs until maybe one day we will have earned the right to give away what we have freely received or to do what God has called us to do. Fortunately God is teaching us a better way.

I had gone to Bible college for several years and was planning to do some more when the Lord said, "Why are you doing that?"

"Because I want to preach the gospel!" I answered enthusiastically. "This is going to open the doors!"

"Really?" He said. And I suddenly recognized the lie I had been believing. I had been approaching the kingdom with a secular mind-set. I had to repent for trying to earn what only God could do.

It isn't that Bible college is wrong, of course. God calls many people down that path. It was a good experience for me and gave me a hunger to learn more and some valuable tools for ministry. But whenever we put anything in the place of God's ways—whenever we say, "I'll do this, and then I'll get that," as though we're the ones solely responsible to make it happen—we enter a heartbreaking road of performance on which nothing we do will ever be good enough. And we substitute our own strategies for God's wisdom.

That's not how the purposes of God unfold in our lives. They unfold when we realize we cannot make it happen and can only declare His faithfulness and trust Him to open doors. "Just tell me what You want to do next, Lord." That's our response to Him. And He promises that His plans for us are going to be fulfilled. "I will cry out to God Most High, to God who performs all things for me"

(Ps. 57:2). When we trust Him, He will accomplish what He purposes.

THE IMPOSSIBLE
BECOMES POSSIBLE

In that place of intimacy with Christ we experience His life within us in increasing power. This is closely related to the resting in the chair we explored earlier. It's His life within us that does the work; we rest in Him and rely on Him to do it. If we try to maintain our position, we begin to wobble in the chair. But do you see how love is related to rest? We have to be able to fully trust that God is on our side and that we are completely in His favor, not because of what we have done to earn it but because of what Jesus has done on our behalf. That trust comes through intimacy, through the close fellowship we have with Him as we sit in His presence.

Then we can do impossible things through Jesus—not just miracles, but also forgiving people who are hard to forgive, loving people who seem unlovely, praying prayers that require great faith, and more. All of those promises of Scripture that we long to step into suddenly become doable because God is able and He lives within us. It doesn't matter how impossible it is to heal the sick, raise the dead, forgive sins, love unconditionally, rejoice in our trials, and so on, if we accept by faith that He is the one doing it in us. We really can live out the dreams He has placed in us no matter how extreme they may seem.

This is where many Christians get stuck. We're still trying to arrive at a place of maturity that qualifies us to fully experience His love and power. Most believers walk around with a guilty conscience because they haven't been perfectly obedient and don't feel qualified to walk in the fulfillment of God's promises. This is one reason so many are afraid to lay hands on the sick and do great exploits for the kingdom. Human reasoning tells us that if we sinned yesterday, we need to wait for a time to pay the price or let our sorrow and repentance really sink in before we are able to enter a level of freedom—which, of course, never comes because we never meet the standards for it.

That's how so many believers feel in God's kingdom. But when God looks at us, He sees the blood of Christ and tells us we're altogether lovely. He finds us spotless and beautiful. We are joined together with Jesus—and what God has joined, let no man separate. What God has called clean, do not call unclean.

My marriage to Tom is a great illustration of this. My husband has earned money through his business, and I get to enjoy it simply because I am married to him. In the same way, we get to enjoy the blessings earned by Jesus, the most wonderful husband in the world. They are all His blessings, but they are ours too. We sit with Him and get to give them away to everyone who needs to experience His goodness.

There is no reason, then, to wait until we are "qualified" to step into the dreams God has given us. It does Him no honor for us to cringe and behave as though we aren't qualified. He already qualified us! Through our intimacy with Him He births His plans in us and begins to manifest them in our lives through our faith and patience. We don't need to sort ourselves out first. In fact, we can't. God didn't create us to navel-gaze, trying in the dark to figure ourselves out. If we buy into that lie, we'll never be ready to go and serve the Lord.

We never arrive at being "problem-free." There will always be stuff, and God isn't looking for us to try and figure it out. He's looking for us to give it to Him. We just come. Somehow He takes out all the anxieties and irritations— things we don't even know are there in the deepest layers of our lives—and fills us with His light. In that place where we begin to believe and trust Him, He'll do as He promised, and we will walk in His glory. He will cover us with His feathers, shelter us with His wings, and make His faithful promises our armor and protection (Ps. 91:4).

God wants you to come in and truly settle down and rest in this faithfulness that He surrounds you with. He wants you to come into the truth of what the gospel says: that you have been raised up with Him, that you are the apple of His eye, seated at the right hand of the Father, sur-rounded by His love. God wants you to walk with a holy confidence. It is only in this place that you can have faith to believe His promises for you will be fulfilled. In that place, where you're surrounded by the love of God, His love sparks faith in your heart to believe the things He has spoken over your life.

◦☙ ♒◦

Maintaining your faith in what He has said can be a battle.

◦☙ ♒◦

If you've tried hard to talk yourself into believing Him, you know how impossible it is to do that on your own. But if you're fully convinced that you're securely seated with

Him—if you're letting yourself come into the fullness of the truth that He really has made you clean and that He really is for you and on your side, and you are keeping these truths continually before your eyes and in your heart— faith will rise up from within you. Let God's dreams be conceived in you and let them rise up, and you will be able to release faith—the faith of Jesus Himself—that receives the promises He has for you.

WAGE WAR
WITH THE PROMISES

You will have to contend for this faith. Your dreams don't just happen accidentally. They do happen as you rest in Him, but it isn't a passive rest. You have to be very resolved and intentional about it. First Timothy 1:18 tells us to wage warfare with the prophetic words spoken over us because it really is a war sometimes. Other people will speak things over you that contradict what God has spoken over you, and they may even ridicule you. Maintaining your faith in what He has said can be a battle.

King David was no stranger to opposition. First Samuel 17 recounts the story of a young David being sent by his father to take supplies to his brothers. When he arrived, he witnessed Goliath's taunts. The giant would come out and challenge the Israelites to send a man out to fight him, saying the Philistines would become Israel's slaves if he lost, but Israel would have to become the Philistines' slaves if he won. Full of faith in the Lord who had always proven Himself faithful, and carrying God's promise spoken through Samuel in his heart, David had a fresh and hope-filled view of the situation the army was facing. God is looking for this response—a new breed that sees challenges as opportunities for miracles.

> Early in the morning David left the flock with a shepherd, loaded up and set out, as Jesse had directed. He reached the camp as the army was going out to its battle positions, shouting the war cry. Israel and the Philistines were drawing up their lines facing each other. David left his things with the keeper of supplies, ran to the battle lines and greeted his brothers. As he was talking with them, Goliath, the Philistine champion from Gath, stepped out from his lines and shouted his usual defiance, and David heard it. When the Israelites saw the man, they all fled from him in great fear.
>
> Now the Israelites had been saying, "Do you see how this man keeps coming out? He comes out to defy Israel. The king will give great wealth to the man who kills him. He will also give him his daughter in marriage and will exempt his family from taxes in Israel." David asked the men standing near him, "What will be done for the man who kills this Philistine and removes this disgrace from Israel? Who is this uncircumcised Philistine that he should defy the armies of the living God?" They repeated to him what they had been saying and told him, "This is what will be done for the man who kills him."
>
> —1 SAMUEL 17:20–27, NIV

David saw the challenge that was causing Israel to tremble in fear as a glorious blessing from God. He had a righteous confidence based on God's covenant with Israel that this was designed to work out for the nation's good. God is for us, so who can be against us? David began to point out that God had promised to be with them and deliver them and that the Philistines had no such covenant.

Eliab, David's older brother, seemed to take offense at David's faith. He began to ridicule his little brother and accuse him of less-than-pure motives.

> Now Eliab his oldest brother heard when he spoke to the men; and Eliab's anger was aroused against David, and he said, "Why did you come down here? And with whom have you left those few sheep in the wilderness? I know your pride and the insolence of your heart, for you have come down to see the battle."
>
> —1 SAMUEL 17:28

It can be so hard when accusations are unfairly made against your heart. For prophetic people who are generally super-sensitive anyway, this can be deeply painful. But the pain is significantly amplified when the attacks come from those you would expect to support you, such as family and those who are older in the faith. David's accuser was his own older brother, and the venom in his words was obviously meant to intimidate, humiliate, and shut David down.

Older brothers and sisters, like the brother in the story of the prodigal son, often struggle with a younger sibling's success and promotion. Leaders can easily fall into the trap of trying to limit those they lead because of their own insecurities. But in the kingdom we reap what we sow. If we promote and celebrate others in their success, we also get to go to another level. In celebrating others, we get caught in the updraft of their promotion. As believers our role is to disciple others to go further than we have, and in doing so, we see the kingdom advance and share in the reward. Just as any good parents want their children to go further and be more successful than they themselves were, we are all called to be mothers and fathers in the faith, rejoicing when our ceiling becomes the next generation's floor. If those we disciple go further than we do, we have been successful.

Eliab's attack was on David's identity. He begins by sarcastically pointing out David's current circumstances. "And with whom have you left those few sheep in the wilderness?" The enemy will always try to remind you of your circumstances, but God wants you to remember His promises. The attack was trying to link David's qualifications to his circumstances. It was as if Eliab were saying, "You are a nobody, you aren't part of the formal army, and you don't even have a uniform. All you do is look after a few sheep! How dare you come here and make us seem cowardly with your faith talk."

In this day of acceleration and awakening, a new breed is coming forth with radical faith based on the knowledge that God really is with them and for them. Perfect love that casts out fear is birthing a faith-filled, fearless generation who will do great exploits, miracles, signs, and wonders. This can be an affront to those who hold to a religious works mentality. Sadly, many times those who have been part of a previous move of God end up persecuting the next move of the Spirit because they have found identity in what they have done rather than in God's great love for them. So when someone does more, it makes them feel less valuable.

The next attack was against David's heart and motives. This can be an even harder thing to handle. Interestingly, Eliab was passed over by Samuel because the Lord said He looked on the heart. Wounded people who don't receive healing wound others. God loved David's heart, and now David had the opportunity of choosing whom he would believe—God or his brother.

I love David's response to this attack.

> And David said, "What have I done now? Is there not a cause?" Then he turned from him toward another and said the same thing; and these people answered him as the first ones did.
> —1 Samuel 17:29–30

Instead of being drawn into a fistfight with his brother or into a retaliatory war of words with him, David responded by focusing on what was important: "Is there not a cause?" Too often we can be caught up in the wrong fight. We need to remember what the call and the cause are and refuse to be distracted by the enemies' taunts. Just as Nehemiah responded to Sanballat—the enemy who kept harassing Nehemiah's work in rebuilding Jerusalem's wall— we need to say to those who want to draw us into flesh-and-blood fights, "I am doing a great work and I cannot come down" (Neh. 6:3, NAS).

We are called to the cause of the kingdom and the good fight of faith. David could have thrown accusations and judgments back at his brother: "You're just jealous of me, and you've never accepted the fact that I've been anointed." He could have tried to publicly embarrass his brother by telling everyone else about how Samuel rejected Eliab.

Or he could have run home to his father to complain

about his brother's words. After all, David had come down to bless his brothers with supplies. When faced with unfair criticism, we often respond by building a case against the other person by judging them or building a team to support us in our judgment of them. If you find yourself in a team that spends time and conversation talking about how bad someone else is or how badly they have behaved, you might be forgetting the real cause you are called to.

Bitter-root judgments never bear good fruit and can seriously sidetrack us. If David had been drawn into a fight with his brother, he may have missed the main event and the destiny God had for him that day. Instead, he turned from Eliab and continued building faith in those around him.

To walk in the miraculous, we must stay focused on the call. God wants us to be careful to take captive any thought that would try to distract us or exalt itself above the knowledge of who He is. If a thought doesn't line up with the thoughts of God, it needs to be rejected, not reacted to. God is our defense and strong tower; the righteous need only to run into Him to stay safe. We must guard our hearts from these distractions and condemnations with great diligence because it's out of our hearts that the life-giving power of God flows.

WE DON'T WRESTLE
FLESH AND BLOOD

I have been tempted to go to war in the flesh sometimes, especially when people speak about my family or those I love. Over and over again in my mind I have often rehearsed speeches of what I think they need to hear, but doing this robs me of peace and leads to judgment and bitterness. I have to go rest in the chair and ask the Lord to let His peace come into my heart. I remind Him of His promise to me and thank Him that no weapon formed against me will prosper. I claim promises such as Revelation 3:9, which tells me my opponents will come and acknowledge that God has loved me.

> His truth is a like a hook on
> which we can hang our faith.

I tell Him, "You've said all my children shall be taught of the Lord, and great shall be the peace of my children. You've promised that the fire would go forth, the deaf would hear, the blind would see, and the lame would walk. You have told me I'll lay hands on the sick and they will recover. This is my inheritance and my destiny, regardless of what anyone else says." I remind myself that God has spoken greater things to me than other people have spoken over me.

We have to be conscious of the warfare going on and fight with the word God has spoken. His truth is a like a hook on which we can hang our faith. When God speaks to you and reveals the dreams He has for you, you can write them down and take them to battle. Declare them. Pray in tongues. When fog and confusion come, speaking out the truth of God will cause haziness to go away. He intercedes through us on our behalf when we pray in the Spirit. And when He has spoken, we have every reason to say, "I'm not letting go until You bless me. I'm not giving up. I'll keep coming after You because You're the one I want." That's what abiding in Him looks like, and abiding will produce much fruit.

Jesus Himself understands the battles we face. The enemy tried to attack Christ's identity when He was in the wilderness (Matt. 4:1–11). Remember, the enemy's temptation began with the statement, "If You are the Son of God…" (v. 3). But Jesus knew who He was and would not let Himself be drawn into having to prove Himself. This attack followed God's announcement at Jesus's baptism that this was His Son in whom He was well pleased (Matt. 3:17). Jesus's identity had just been openly declared.

Likewise, because you are in Christ, you have no need to strive or work to establish your identity as God's beloved. Now it is no longer you who live but Christ who lives in you, so you are also the beloved of God, and the Father is well pleased with you. You have nothing to prove. Miracles flow because of your identity, not as evidence to establish your identity. Jesus had done no major miracles when God declared His love and pleasure for Him. In the same way God is pleased with you and calls you His beloved not based on what you have done but because of your faith in Christ's great grace.

David didn't question whether God was on his side.

> Now when the words which David spoke were heard, they reported them to Saul; and he sent for him. Then David said to Saul, "Let no man's heart fail because of him; your servant will go and fight with this Philistine."
>
> —1 SAMUEL 17:31–32

Only someone who had confidence in God and a solid belief that God had no problem using him could respond as David did to Saul. The world is longing for this, for sons and daughters of God to manifest the Savior, for believers who know that Christ in them is the hope of glory. Too often Christians shrink back and look for someone else to do the "big stuff." When you know God is for you and that the same Spirit that was on Jesus is on you, and you believe God has qualified you by His great love and amazing grace, you will also have confidence to believe that when a negative circumstance arises, Jesus in you is the answer ready to help. Instead of having you look for someone else to lead your friend to Christ or to release healing to them, God wants to awaken you to the truth that He in you is the answer waiting to manifest through you.

STOP GIVING AWAY OPPORTUNITIES!

Many years ago I received a request from a friend in the United States, asking if I had a word for France, as he was heading there to minister. I remember thinking to myself, "Who can I ask to prophesy over France?" My mentor was overseas, and it never occurred to me that I should ask the Lord for a word, as I had never prophesied over a country before. As I was having these thoughts, the Lord spoke to me and said, "Stop giving away the opportunities I give you."

Up until then I didn't see myself as qualified to speak to nations. Like the Israelite spies, I felt like a grasshopper in my own sight. But God wants us to see ourselves not in the light of what we've done but in view of His love for us and who He has called us to be. So I went and got a recorder and began to prophesy over France. I also had a word for my friend's ministry. When he and his wife read the word, he said they felt the glory in the room, and they promptly invited me to come to the United States to minister. Only weeks earlier I had received a prophetic word that God was going to open doors in the United States, and here was God doing just as He had promised. God is faithful and only looks for our obedience.

PROPHETIC COUNCIL

A few years ago I felt the Lord prompt me to gather the prophets in our nation and establish a national council. I had hoped for years that someone would initiate something like this but had not imagined myself doing it. So when God spoke to me that day in my living room, I once again had to adjust my view. To my delight the response around the nation was wonderful, and today we have a beautiful unity developing among the prophetic voices of the nation.

God has great plans for you, but you must be prepared to allow Him to help you enlarge your capacity to dream.

> As it is written: "Eye has not seen, nor ear heard, nor have entered into the heart of man the things which God has prepared for those who love Him." But God has revealed them to us through His Spirit. For the Spirit searches all things, yes, the deep things of God. For what man knows the things of a man except the spirit of the man which is in him? Even so no one knows the things of God except the Spirit

of God. Now we have received, not the spirit of
the world, but the Spirit who is from God, that
we might know the things that have been freely
given to us by God.

—1 CORINTHIANS 2:9–12

God wants to share the big, miraculous plans He has
for you by the power of His Spirit, enabling you to dream
with Him and conceive His great purposes.

David must have been dreaming with God as he col-
lected those stones to fight Goliath. Look at what he said
to Goliath before the battle:

Then David said to the Philistine, "You come to
me with a sword, with a spear, and with a jav-
elin. But I come to you in the name of the LORD
of hosts, the God of the armies of Israel, whom
you have defied. This day the LORD will deliver
you into my hand, and I will strike you and take
your head from you. And this day I will give the
carcasses of the camp of the Philistines to the
birds of the air and the wild beasts of the earth,
that all the earth may know that there is a God
in Israel. Then all this assembly shall know that
the LORD does not save with sword and spear;
for the battle is the LORD's, and He will give
you into our hands."

—1 SAMUEL 17:45–47

David must have been allowing the Lord to write on
the screen of his imagination in order to declare so confidently what would happen. Instead of preparing for the
confrontation with Goliath by entertaining thoughts of
possible negative outcomes and allowing fear to set in,

David rehearsed in faith what he was hoping for. Hope is a joyful expectation of things that are not yet seen with natural eyes but with the eyes of the Spirit within you. "Faith is the substance of things hoped for, the evidence of things not seen" (Heb. 11:1). David spoke out what he had already seen in his heart.

Fear not! The only weapon the enemy can use against you is deception, and he wants to fill you with fear and doubt. The only hope the enemy has is to try to get you to doubt the faithfulness of God and attempt to work things out in some other way. That's why you need to get deliberate and say, "No. I will not fear. Who can be against me? My God will do all things He has promised." As you rest in His faithfulness, His favor surrounds you like a shield. You can get out from behind it and try to fight your own battles if you want, but it's so much better to let Him cover you. He is absolutely magnificent in the way He fights His battles on our behalf.

BELIEVING BELIEVERS

I believe that in this current awakening God is making believers into actual believers—people who truly, deeply believe. I see it as an entire culture shift within the church. God isn't just pouring out His Spirit to entertain us; He wants to capture our hearts and propel us forward.

Knowing His love enables us to have faith, and faith is the key to everything we receive from God. He has laid before us a banqueting table. We can freely come and eat of it. We don't need to hope for a revelation; we can ask and expect to receive one. We don't need to wish for an encounter with Him; we can go and get one in faith. We aren't left only to dream of miracles; we can count on walking in them.

~··~··~·

He wants to capture our hearts and propel us forward.

~··~··~·

We can know God is dreaming through us, praying through us, working through us, and laying that path out in front of us. Doing all these things without faith doesn't accomplish much, but pursuing them in faith is more powerful than we can imagine. When we sit at the right hand of the Father, secure in His love, we are fruitful in that place and able to exercise the glorious authority we've been given. We are now coheirs of every promise Jesus has been given.

We don't have to earn the right to receive those promises. We work and serve the Lord out of the overflow of His love that He continually offers us. He wants each one of us to walk around with the sense that we are incredibly special. Some might think we'll become arrogant if we let that message sink in, but the truth is that if we allow God to love us at the level He wants to, our hearts won't become proud. They will bow down in amazement at how good He is.

The more you let God tell you you're special—that you have a destiny and that you're going to change the world—the more He will use you to bring His glory through you. And the more you will step into your dreams and really believe them. You will grow more and more humble as you recognize what He is doing in your life and that it really is Him, not your own ability to make things happen.

God has created you to dream His dreams, and His dreams are supernatural and miraculous. Allow Him to take you into supernatural daydreams as you fellowship with Him, and conceive His magnificent plans for your life.

Chapter 10

PROPHETIC ADVENTURES

The Joy of Prophetic Intercession

Y EARS AGO I was having dinner with friends when I suddenly felt an urgent impulse to pray. I wasn't fearful at all. I just felt a really strong pull from the Holy Spirit to separate myself and pray. Fortunately my friends understood, and I excused myself.

As I knelt down to pray, I found myself taken into an all-encompassing vision. I saw a street in Germany and could describe the sidewalk and the shop fronts as clearly as if I was there, even though I had never been to Germany. At the time my husband was in Stuttgart on business, and I sensed he needed prayer support. I began to pray in the Spirit for about fifteen minutes. Then the vision was over and the burden lifted.

When I called Tom the next day, I told him what had happened and described the urgency I'd felt to pray and the place where the Lord had taken me. As it turns out, that was exactly where he was at the time I had prayed, and he had had an urgent need for prayer right at the moment God had called me away from the dinner table. He was amazed when he heard me describe what I had seen.

After this, these calls to intercession became more

common. I felt an urgency to pray for a friend a few nights later. I felt as though the Lord took me in the Spirit to a parking lot where I saw my friend in a car with a man and felt that there was some danger for her. When I spoke with her about it the next day, I found out that she had been in a car with a man the night before and had been very close to giving into temptation but had found the strength to say no to him before it was too late.

I didn't have any knowledge or suspicion of what sort of danger she was in when I was praying; I didn't even know she was seeing someone. I was so blessed to see how the Lord is not out to embarrass anyone, but He does allow people who seek His heart to be involved in praying for those He loves. God wants to move us with His compassion too so we can flow in the supernatural.

These sorts of encounters became more regular as I began to recognize and understand the importance of responding to the gentle pull of the Holy Spirit to prayer. At times I would be driving and have to pull over onto the side of the road to pray as I was taken up in the Spirit for prophetic intercession. At other times I would feel the need to separate myself to give myself to His pull while He would show me visions of things to come.

Prophetic intercession is a glorious joy as we partner with God in His care for people. In her book *The Voice of God: How God Speaks Personally and Corporately to His Children Today* Cindy Jacobs writes that you can be an intercessor and not be a prophet, but you can't be a prophet and not be an intercessor. I agree with her. Unless a prophet has a heart to intercede in love for people, he or she will never fully enter the office of prophet because true prophecy is an overflow of love for God and His people. As

1 Corinthians 13:2 says, if you prophesy but have not love, you are nothing.

As I've shared, there have been times when people have started being healed before I could pray for them. To my surprise, the words of knowledge I have for people in some meetings are only to declare the miracles that God has already done a few minutes earlier. I once had a word of knowledge that a woman's hips were being healed. A woman responded, saying that just before I had given the word, she had felt something like electricity suddenly hit her and heal her. She responded to the word of knowledge by simply demonstrating how she could now walk and do other things she couldn't previously do without pain.

This is something God has done repeatedly. Recently some brothers came to a meeting asking for prayer for another brother, who was in intensive care. As we prayed, I felt the Lord take me into the intensive care unit and lay hands on him, and I prayed and released healing. Within minutes of finishing our prayer, one of the brothers received a phone call saying the young man had opened his eyes.

The Lord never embarrasses people
but will always use the revelatory
gifts to reveal His love for them.

These sorts of experiences are not a new thing. The healing minister John G. Lake also recorded a similar experience when he was in South Africa. He was in a meeting in Johannesburg reading a prayer request when, moved with compassion, he knelt down on the platform to pray. He said he felt himself being lifted up and flying over the continent, seeing the different nations as he flew over them until he became aware that he was in a village in Wales. Then he saw a public building that he recognized as an asylum.

The door was opened, and he went into a room where a woman was lying in bed restrained, shaking her head and muttering incoherently. He laid his hands on her head, cast the demon spirit out of her in the name of Jesus Christ, and released healing to her. He observed her face soften and change and knew she had been healed. All the while he was still on the platform in Johannesburg praying as the congregation joined him in earnest prayer. Three weeks later they received the report that this woman who had been confined for seven years had suddenly been healed.

Today I am continuously overjoyed as the Lord ministers prophetically through believers with words of love, hope, and destiny. Just as He taught me in my intercessory adventures, He never embarrasses people but will always use the revelatory gifts to reveal His love for them. The Holy Spirit wants to provoke His people to worship and holiness by revealing to them the truth that they are righteous because of their faith in Him alone. The prophetic ministry is a tool He often uses to encourage people to walk in this calling.

I remember when I first felt the Lord giving me a prophetic word to deliver at church. I was in my early twenties, and I felt as though I had butterflies in my stomach. I urgently prayed that God would confirm to me if He really wanted me to bring this word. So when opportunity was given for people to prophesy, the associate pastor got up and shared the word the Lord had given me. I asked again, "Please, Lord, confirm it again." Another person got up and gave a very similar word. At last I jumped up and echoed what had been said.

◌ↄↄ ↄↄ ◌

God is interested in every area of our lives and loves to speak into our lives to encourage us.

◌ↄↄ ↄↄ ◌

The next week I again felt the Holy Spirit prompt me to prophesy. I immediately asked Him to confirm that He wanted me to share it, and I heard Him ask me why I wouldn't just get up and give the word when the pastor gave the opportunity. It made me think of Jeremiah. The Lord initially showed him some visions and asked him what he saw, and after saying what he saw, the Lord sent him out to prophesy to the nation. God often moves so much faster than we are comfortable with!

One of the things that gives my heart great joy is when the Lord speaks to people through a prophetic word or a word of knowledge. Often a personal prophetic word is a combination of the revelatory gifts, with God giving a word of knowledge about someone's circumstance, a word of prophecy about His future plans, and words of wisdom about how to cooperate with His plan. God is interested in every area of our lives and loves to speak into our lives to encourage us. Often the Lord has had me prophesy unknowingly over people who are just visiting church and who don't know Him, and I get so excited when they experience the love He speaks to them and they open their hearts to Christ.

I remember ministering one night to a Muslim man who had walked into one of our meetings late, having missed the message entirely. I didn't know he was Muslim or anything else about him when the Lord told me to call him out. I began to prophesy about him having pieces of a jigsaw puzzle and how the Lord loved him and wanted to help him make sense of the pieces so he could see the full picture. I don't remember what else I said, but I do remember the impact it had on him. We gave him a recording of the word he had received, and the next week he came back to tell us that he had listened to it twenty times and had played it to his Muslim family because he was so astonished that God would feel that way about him. To hear that God loved him so impacted him that it turned him into an evangelist for Christ.

Other times the Lord will show me what people do for a living or speak to me about their loved ones or their deepest concerns. It unlocks hearts in such an amazing way. All of these sorts of prophecies testify to the love God has for people, and whether a person is a believer or not, a true word from God can impact a heart so deeply that it turns a life around.

That's why we love to minister on the streets. A word of knowledge or a miracle always gets people's attention. Then when we have their attention, we have an open door to prophesy and share the good news of the gospel. I love to watch people's countenance as words of knowledge coupled with hope grab their attention and light up their eyes. As Paul said, it is not persuasive words of man's wisdom but demonstrations of the Spirit's power that gets the job done.

The gifts of God testify to and reveal the nature and character of our amazing, loving God. The testimony of

Jesus is the spirit of prophecy, and throughout the Gospels Jesus always manifested Himself as the answer the world needed. So prophecy should have embedded in it the testimony of Jesus, who is still the answer and the desire of the nations. I cringe when I hear so-called prophetic words that declare doom and gloom over people or nations while offering them no hope or instruction and failing to point people to Jesus. We must be careful not to misrepresent the heart of God for the world He has died to redeem.

I've been in meetings where people have walked out when the prophecies begin, afraid that God would pick them out and reveal their sins. There is an accuser of the brethren, but this accuser is not a prophet or the Holy Spirit. He is the enemy of our souls, out to condemn us. More often than not I've found that it's the goodness and kindness of God that leads people to repentance. Everything we do must be done in love as God moves us with His compassion, just as Jesus was moved with compassion and healed all who came to Him.

On rare occasions God has given me words that relate to issues in people's lives, but it has nearly always been something I have shared in a private setting. The first time this happened, I was ministering at the altar and was praying for a man when the Lord showed me a vision of beer. I began asking the Lord what beer represented, thinking that there must be some encouraging word in the vision, but I didn't get any interpretation. So I didn't share it with him and asked the Lord for another vision, which I did share.

It seemed to be a blessing to him, so I naïvely shared with him the first vision without any judgment or suspicion in my heart. His reaction really surprised me. He started to cry and shared that he had been really struggling with an addiction to beer and wanted to get free but was too ashamed to seek help. So we prayed there and then, and the Lord set him free. I don't believe he felt any judgment or condemnation from the word, and God simply allowed it to be given privately in order to answer the cry in his heart for freedom and to show him that God loved him and wanted to help him.

A similar thing happened with another man I received a vision for during an altar call. I saw a horse race and began asking the Lord what it meant. I struggled to find an interpretation, genuinely thinking that maybe it was about running the Christian race or something like that. As I shared it privately with him, he gave a sigh of relief and said he had a problem with gambling on horse races. Again, God used it as an opportunity to set him free.

THE TREASURE INSIDE

I must point out, though, that these sorts of prophecies are not the norm. We have to be very careful and sensitive—and very discreet—if God gives us a word that could possibly embarrass someone. No one should enjoy bringing correction, and it should always be done with humility, honor, and love. More often than not God will declare destiny over people, calling out the treasure on the inside of them and awakening them to their new nature in Christ. Most people are well aware of their faults, but they don't know how loved and treasured they are or how good God's plan for their lives is. God shares His secrets with His friends the prophets, but the prophets must be lovers who overflow with His love in order to effectively reveal the heart of the One speaking.

We are created in the image of the God who created the world with His words, so we must be so careful to speak words of life. We need to seek God for His way of delivery and His interpretation, always being aware that when dealing with people, we are dealing with the apple of His eye. To be filled with all the fullness of God is to overflow, and with that overflow comes love-empowered signs and wonders. Prophecy and prophetic intercession will flow like a river from a heart overflowing with love.

I received a word regarding my songwriting when I was quite young, and it brings home the importance of delivering a word in love so that it releases life. I had just started writing songs when a man called me out of a crowd to give me a word. He proceeded to say that he had seen a vision of a clock at a quarter past the hour and then gave his interpretation. He said that my songwriting was one-quarter anointed and three-quarters un-anointed.

Prophecy and prophetic intercession will flow like a river from a heart overflowing with love.

I was devastated! I went home and certainly didn't want to pick up a pencil and write anymore. If instead the word had been delivered out of an overflow of God's loving heart, grounded in a revelation of His grace, I would have reacted very differently. The same vision could have been delivered like this: "I see that the Lord has anointed you to write songs, and it is His desire to increase that anointing threefold." Such a delivery would have inspired me to run home and write. The same word delivered two different ways can have vastly different impacts.

God encourages all of us to eagerly desire the prophetic gift. First Corinthians 14:1 says, "Pursue love, and desire spiritual gifts, but especially that you may prophesy." The gift of prophecy is a powerful tool to release hope and faith, so it's understandable that the apostle Paul encourages all believers to pursue the gift and grow in it. We have seen that the hope released from a prophetic word literally saves lives.

A few years ago a man from Australia was diagnosed with terminal bladder cancer and given three months to live. He began to search the Internet looking for ministers who had prayed for cancer victims and found a video testimony. Inspired with hope, he came to one of our meetings.

That Friday night he introduced himself to me. Unbeknownst to me, he felt that if I called him out by name to pray, then he would be healed. Partway through the service, I felt the Holy Spirit prompt me to call him to come for prayer. He was so excited; to him that was the confirmation he was waiting for to know he would be healed. The Lord gave me a prophetic word about his future, and we released healing to him. He was ecstatic with joy and left the meeting that night full of faith to return home.

When he went to the doctor to confirm his healing, he was told that while his condition had improved, he was still in the final stages of cancer and nothing more could be done. But this man was holding on to the word he received about his future. In the following weeks, even as he was in severe pain, he continued to declare the prophetic word spoken over him and the fact that he had been healed. Six months later he wrote to us to say that his condition had improved even more. He was alive and well and praising God.

༺ ~ ༻

Pursue prophecy. It's a life-giving gift and glorious revelation of God's love for people.

༺ ~ ༻

I love it when we see immediate results, as we often do, but I love this story because of the beauty of this man's hope-filled journey of faith. Prophecy is a powerful weapon to wage war with! Consider Joseph: he had a prophetic promise from God based on a series of dreams he had; if he had allowed circumstances to dictate his belief, he would have lost hope.

> He sent a man before them, even Joseph, who was sold as a servant. His feet they hurt with fetters; he was laid in chains of iron and his soul entered into the iron, until his word [to his cruel brothers] came true, until the word of the Lord tried and tested him.
> —Psalm 105:17–19, AMP

A prophetic promise from the Lord is like a hook for your faith and is something with which you can spiritually wage war. David waged that kind of war when he was being pursued in the wilderness. He wrote, "I would have despaired unless I had believed that I would see the goodness of the LORD in the land of the living" (Ps. 27:13, NAS).

He held on in hope to the promise of God spoken prophetically to him through Samuel and Jonathan. So pursue prophecy. It's a life-giving gift and glorious revelation of God's love for people.

I love that the apostle Paul links the desire to prophesy to the pursuit of love in 1 Corinthians 13. Love is always the motivation to prophesy, to work miracles, and to release healing. Without it Christ is not revealed or glorified. The power gifts testify to His nature, and He is love.

> Two blind men sitting by the road, hearing that Jesus was passing by, cried out, "Lord, have mercy on us, Son of David!" The crowd sternly told them to be quiet, but they cried out all the more, "Lord, Son of David, have mercy on us!" And Jesus stopped and called them, and said, "What do you want Me to do for you?" They said to Him, "Lord, we want our eyes to be opened." Moved with compassion, Jesus touched their eyes; and immediately they regained their sight and followed Him.
>
> —MATTHEW 20:30–34, NAS

Jesus was moved with compassion, and He healed them. Power still flows on God's compassionate love. We must have God's heart of love for the ones we are ministering to if we want to see His power flow. His desire, regardless of whether we are prophesying or releasing healing, is that the one receiving encounters His great love for them.

TO THE STREETS!

I now mentor teams of people who are passionate about prophesying and giving words of knowledge on the streets and in hospitals or wherever they can find people who need to encounter God's love. As a result, people are being saved and healed, blind eyes are opening and deaf ears hearing, and new believers are being baptized. It's love for God that drives these people, and it's the love of God demonstrated in signs and wonders that leads people to Christ. Instead of encountering religion that tells them what is wrong with them, people are being joyfully surprised by grace that transforms their world.

We have started a ministry school through our church that takes students to the streets every week as part of their course, and it is a delight to watch and see how much joy they have as they experience God stepping through them supernaturally. The revelatory and power gifts are mighty expressions of God's heart and can break down any walls of resistance that may have been constructed in people's hearts. God delights to tell people how He sees them—that they are His children and that He loves them with an everlasting love.

The Lord is raising up a mighty army, and each person has a destiny in Him. He wants you to be fulfilling yours now. It may take some time for things to unfold, but He wants you to be stepping toward that destiny. He doesn't want you to wait until "one day" when you finally feel you're ready to minister because you've attained some kind of qualification you don't already have. He wants you to believe the dreams He has given you and begin walking in them now.

If you know what God has been calling you to do, begin to say, "Lord, what do You want me to do now?" Recognize that the times we are living in are not a dress rehearsal. The great awakening that is unfolding now is the real thing. Many have released prophetic words that cause a stir and put the church in a tailspin, but God's perspective is much more hopeful than that. We live in exciting times. There is a tsunami coming, not of judgment but of God's glory. And it will be wonderful.

We have a lot of surfers in Australia, and they know what to do when a wave starts to swell. You position yourself and start to swim. God wants us to ride this wave with Him—to recognize what is happening and start swimming, to focus on Him without getting distracted. This is not a time to sleep; the wave of revival has only just begun. It's going to get amazingly glorious.

Chapter 11

EMBRACING GOD'S FAITHFULNESS

Awakenings and the Greater Story

A s I'VE TRAVELED, it has surprised me to realize that many people don't know much about the spiritual awakenings that are such a significant aspect of Christian history. The momentum of history is so much a part of this last great awakening that it's well worth going through a basic outline of past moves of God. Seeing what God has done throughout history positions us to better recognize the awakening that is upon us and take advantage of the greater wave that is coming.

AWAKENINGS

> At the hands of the apostles many signs and wonders were taking place among the people; and they were all with one accord in Solomon's portico.... And all the more believers in the Lord, multitudes of men and women, were constantly added to their number, to such an extent that they even carried the sick out into the streets and laid them on cots and pallets,

so that when Peter came by at least his shadow might fall on any one of them. Also the people from the cities in the vicinity of Jerusalem were coming together, bringing people who were sick or afflicted with unclean spirits, and they were all being healed.

—ACTS 5:12, 14–16, NAS

We've seen that when Jesus walked the earth, He healed all who came to Him, never turning anyone away or implying that anyone would be better off by remaining sick. He didn't heal everyone who needed healing—think of the pool of Bethesda in John 5 where there were many sick people, for example—so plenty of needs remained among the people. But according to all four Gospels, every person who came to Him for healing was made whole.

Jesus commissioned His disciples to heal the sick and tell those who were made whole that the kingdom of God had come upon them. Before His death Jesus told His disciples, "Truly, truly, I say to you, he who believes in Me, the works that I do, he will do also; and greater works than these he will do; because I go to the Father" (John 14:12, NAS).

After the glorious outpouring of the Holy Spirit on the Day of Pentecost, the disciples, now clothed with the Spirit of Christ, went out in His name preaching the good news and healing the sick. According to Acts 5:14–16, *all* who came to them were healed—just as they were during Jesus's ministry. This was the standard after the outpouring of the Holy Spirit on that glorious day in the upper room.

Revelation Lost

Sadly, though, as time went on, there was a tragic decline in revelation, relationship with God, and supernatural power. The church was institutionalized and organized, intimate relationship with God was replaced with man-made regulations, and worship was reduced to rituals. Eventually church leaders decided that people couldn't be trusted to interpret what the Bible said, and they would punish anyone other than a priest who was found in possession of a Bible. Mass was conducted only in Latin so the uneducated people couldn't understand what was being said. People's knowledge of Scripture was limited to what they could glean from the stained-glass windows of the church cathedrals. Revelation began to be slowly and tragically replaced by superstition until the world sank into the misery of the Dark Ages.

Glimmers of Hope

Gradually glimmers of light began to appear in the late 1300s. John Wycliffe, a man who came to be known as the morning star of the Reformation, began to question the pope's authority to deny people access to the Word of God in their own language. Under threat of excommunication, around 1380 Wycliffe began a translation of the Bible from Latin into the common English language. Wycliffe died before his translation was complete; his friend John Purvey helped complete the version of the Wycliffe Bible we have today. Though the church hierarchy had hoped Wycliffe's plans to translate the Bible would die with him and burned most of his work, copies continued to circulate, bringing light and revelation to a hungry world.[1]

In 1510 a priest by the name of Martin Luther was shocked on a pilgrimage to Rome by the corruption he witnessed among the clergy. An earlier pope had determined to increase church revenue for his building projects by doing things such as imposing a license on brothels and a special tax on priests who kept mistresses. Another fund-raising concept that was particularly repulsive to Luther involved the practice of selling indulgences for the misdeeds of the dead.[2]

People were told that by buying a paper certificate ratified by the pope for a fee, the souls of their deceased relatives could be set free from purgatory. This became so widespread that you could even buy an indulgence to keep a mistress![3] The practice played on the naivety of the uneducated masses who had no ability to study the Word for themselves, and the selling of indulgences became a very lucrative enterprise for the church hierarchy.

REFORMATION

Disillusioned, Luther began to search the Scriptures for answers, and in 1517 he came to the glorious revelation of justification by faith. He realized how far the church had departed from the simplicity of the gospel of Christ— that Jesus's death completely paid for our sins and by faith alone are we saved. With this as the centerpiece of his message, Luther nailed his *Ninety-Five Theses* to the door of the Wittenberg church. He unwittingly sparked a revolution that would come to be known as the Protestant Reformation.[4] A great awakening came into full swing.

Luther went on to write many papers and embarked on a translation of the Bible into German.[5] Through the efforts of men like Martin Luther and William Tyndale, the Word was released to people in their own languages and, aided by the invention of the printing press, was widely distributed. Reformation had begun, revelation was being received, and the awakening could not be stopped.

With access to the Bible, the momentum of revelation and awakening increased. Anabaptists began to receive revelations about baptism, and the Quakers' experiences with the Holy Spirit as well as numerous other great moves of God were in themselves spiritual awakenings with dramatic consequences. People all across Europe and the rest of Christendom were empowered. As they began to know truth, truth began to set them free.

MORAVIAN REVIVAL

Influenced by the labors and martyrdom of the Bohemian revivalist John Huss, the Moravians were a group of young people who found refuge from persecution on Count Zinzendorf's estate. Nikolaus Ludwig, count and lord of Zinzendorf, was just a young man himself, twenty-seven years old, when the revivalists established on his estate Herrnhut—"the Lord's Watch." The community was a mix of Moravian Brethren, Lutherans, and Reformed Baptists. They argued and had fierce debates about baptism, holiness, and predestination until in July 1727, Count Zinzendorf asked them all to sign a covenant urging them "to seek out and emphasize the points in which they agreed."[6]

The count was a man of prayer and encouraged them all to join together in regular prayer and worship, and to repent and pray that Christ would make them one. Prayer and worship gatherings were arranged, and a deep desire for God grew in all the people. A few weeks later in one of these gatherings, a pastor was overcome by God and sank down into the dust under the power of the Holy Spirit. The prayer meeting went on until midnight. Then on August 13, 1727, they were gathered together for Communion when they were all sovereignly baptized with the Holy Ghost and fire. Many signs and wonders and miracles were reported among them, and a fire for evangelism led them to send out missionaries with great zeal.[7]

Many times they would burn their ships upon arrival on the mission field, choosing to dedicate their lives to preaching the gospel. Their cry was, "May the Lamb that was slain receive the reward of His suffering."[8] William Carey, known as the father of modern missions, was spurred to action by the zeal of the Moravians, who by the time he emerged in ministry had sent out dozens of missionaries.[9]

It is interesting to note that many of the manifestations that were the catalysts for revivals such as the one that occurred among the Moravians are happening in our meetings today. I think the key was that when people recognized God was sovereignly moving, they gave their full attention to what He was doing and turned aside from their normal routines to move with Him. Like Moses, who turned aside when he saw the burning bush, these people turned aside from their daily lives to focus on what God was doing.

The Scriptures tell us that when the Lord saw that Moses turned aside to look intently at the bush (at what God was doing), He spoke to him, and it led to Moses's being commissioned for a great work (Exod. 3). I believe God is trying to get our attention in this generation, as He wants to commission us and demonstrate His glory through us. Lift up your heads, O ye gates, that the King of glory may come in (Ps. 24:9)! As we, the gates of God on earth, lift up our gaze to Him and give Him our full attention, He will come in and do exceedingly more than we could even imagine.

THE GREAT AWAKENINGS

In the eighteenth century God used Jonathan Edwards and George Whitefield to set Protestant Europe and the colonies of British America ablaze with revival. In a movement known as the First Great Awakening, masses were swept into the kingdom with powerful preaching about the need to receive personal salvation. There were reports of people trembling and shaking under the power of God as they were gripped by revelation.[10]

Many of the manifestations that were the catalysts
for revivals are happening in our meetings today.

A man by the name of John Wesley had been converted in a Moravian meeting in England after witnessing the joy and peace of some Moravians aboard a ship on which he had traveled. The ship was in danger of sinking, and everyone, including Wesley, was terrified, except for these Moravians who prayed and worshipped. Their impact on Wesley's life convinced him that they knew God and he didn't, so on his return to England he found a Moravian fellowship.[11]

Before he met the Moravians, John Wesley was an Anglican minister and Christian theologian.[12] After his conversion, John and his brother, Charles, began open-air preaching that sparked widespread revival. The brothers are considered the founders of the Methodist movement, and their passion is credited with providing seeds for the holiness movement and modern Pentecostalism.[13] This move of God contributed to the conversion of many great reformers like William Wilberforce, who is credited with ending the slave trade.[14]

Then in the early nineteenth century, an even larger revival movement, now known as the Second Great Awakening, swept across the United States. Camp meetings such as the Cane Ridge Revival in Kentucky in 1801 attracted as many as twenty thousand people.[15] Witnesses recorded seeing scores of people speaking with new tongues or being suddenly seized with spasms that "unexpectedly dashed them to the ground."[16] Baptists, Methodists, Anglicans, Presbyterians, Congregationalists, and those from the Reformed church all experienced revival during this time. Great preachers such as Charles Finney traveled across the United States, fanning the awakening into flame.[17]

The American Civil War interrupted what is officially known as the Third Great Awakening, which essentially began as a prayer movement in 1857. After the war Dwight L. Moody and the great hymn writer Ira Sankey had a tremendous influence and saw a reigniting of the revival.[18] In Britain, William and Catherine Booth, both Methodist lay preachers, founded the Christian Revival Society, which later became known as the Salvation Army.[19]

SPARKS OF REVIVAL

Late in the 1800s people began to experience the power of the Holy Spirit with dramatic signs and wonders through the ministry of a housewife by the name of Maria Woodworth-Etter. People were again said to be speaking with new tongues and having glorious encounters with God. Secular newspapers documented some of the astonishing miracles that took place in Maria's meetings, and people across the United States began talking about the miracle-working power of God. Missing limbs grew, and people in the meetings were taken into heavenly trances and visions, coming out of them converted and prophesying with great power.[20] Maria Woodworth-Etter's *Diary of Signs and Wonders* provided so much encouragement to me in my early days of ministry, and she is still one of my great heroes of the faith.

So the awakenings continued as the sparks of revival flashed around the world. In 1904 under the leadership of Evan Roberts, approximately one hundred thousand people made commitments to Christ in Wales during the Welsh Revival. Pubs and gambling houses closed down, and police found themselves with little to do as the crime rate dropped. Miners had to retrain their horses, because the horses were used to responding to directions laced with foul language, and the miners no longer spoke that way.[21]

In 1906, as the revival spread to the United States, William Seymour, a one-eyed African American son of former slaves, was used to spark a worldwide Pentecostal awakening that became known as the Azusa Street Revival. Stories are told of a glory cloud that often manifested so visibly in the room of the Azusa Street mission in Los Angeles that children would play hide-and-seek in it. Limbs grew out, and many other amazing signs and wonders were reported and published in newspapers. It was reported that one night the fire department came rushing in to put out a fire, only to find that the flames they saw on the top of the building were supernatural.[22]

With the fresh outpouring of the Holy Ghost came accelerated revelation of God's healing power. Men such as John Alexander Dowie and John G. Lake also arose in the wake of Maria Woodworth-Etter and demonstrated the power of God as they healed the sick and raised the dead.

Lake went with his family to South Africa and saw God do remarkable things. Many of the miracles have been documented in his book *Adventures With God*. He went on to found the Healing Rooms in Spokane, Washington. As a result, Spokane became known as the healthiest city in the United States.

A British plumber named Smith Wigglesworth began to see astounding miracles after his baptism in the Holy Spirit. Evangelist Aimee Semple McPherson took up her Foursquare gospel and helped advance worldwide revival through her radio broadcasts and large healing meetings.

During the 1950s amazing miracles happened on a vast scale, with Gordon Lindsay documenting miracles during what was to become known as the Voice of Healing revival. Oral Roberts and others began to hold huge tent meetings, and the word of knowledge and prophecy began to be demonstrated with glorious healings and miracles. William Branham, Paul Cain, Jack Coe, and A. A. Allen were among the many who embraced the message of healing with amazing demonstrations of the Holy Spirit's power.

During the late sixties and seventies Kathryn Kuhlman became a household name as her books and radio programs documented testimonies of dramatic healings and miracles being performed by the Holy Spirit. Television spread the word further, and innumerable people testified that they were healed. But Kuhlman struggled to understand why some were healed and others weren't. Happily she chose not to lower her doctrine to the level of her experience but to simply believe God's Word.[23]

As revelation continues to increase,
healings and miracles are being seen
every day all over the world.

In the early seventies God was moving powerfully. The Catholic charismatic renewal began in 1967 at a retreat at a Catholic university in Pittsburgh. Many Catholics were baptized in the Holy Spirit and spoke in tongues, and a renewed passion for the gifts of the Holy Spirit such as healing was sparked. University campuses became a hotbed of revival, and many young people involved in the hippie movement were brought to Christ.[24] What came to be known as the Jesus People movement saw young men and women from all walks of life come to Christ in huge numbers as the Holy Spirit supernaturally moved on hearts, causing them to cry out for truth.

The Jesus People held a firm belief in signs, wonders,

miracles, faith, healing, prayer, and the Bible. It was a movement marked by the Holy Spirit with signs and wonders, and it was a time of fruitful harvest. Many of today's leaders were converted during that time, including Mike Bickle, Bob Hartley, Ché Ahn, Lance Wallnau, and Charles Stock. You can read Charles Stock's story in his book *Glow in the Dark*.

Today, as revelation continues to increase, healings and miracles are being seen every day all over the world. Reinhard Bonnke, founder of Christ for all Nations, is literally seeing millions dramatically healed and saved in his international crusades. In Africa, during one crusade alone, one million people came to a saving knowledge of Christ.[25] Africa is awakening to the good news as the gospel is being preached and confirmed with signs and wonders.

In 1993–1994 a move of God began to sweep the earth, and Toronto Airport Christian Fellowship in Canada came to international attention. What became known as the "Toronto Blessing" radically impacted the modern charismatic church. Joy and revelation of the Father's heart swept through the church around the world, and people experienced great freedom as they came to the truth of the Father's love for them.[26] Subsequent revivals, like one that began at Brownsville Assembly of God in Pensacola, Florida, saw thousands come to Christ and later spread around the world.[27] In Toronto, leaders such as Bill Johnson and Heidi and Rolland Baker had radical encounters with God and have gone on to have a glorious impact around the globe.

Heidi and Rolland Baker, founders of Iris Ministries, were in their own words "miserable missionaries," running a small mission and orphanage in Mozambique. Feeling utterly burned out, they went to Toronto, where a revival was in full swing. Heidi encountered God in a powerful way as He spoke to her about the unreached tribes of Africa. She was dramatically baptized with the fire and joy of God, and was unable to walk for seven days as the glory of God washed over her.[28]

Heidi and Rolland have gone on to overcome huge obstacles and plant thousands of churches in Africa after their experience in Toronto. Now they are well on their way to reaching their goal of adopting one million orphans into their Iris Ministries family. They are seeing God raise people from the dead and quadriplegics miraculously being able to run as the Holy Spirit heals them. Millions are being fed naturally and spiritually as the Holy Spirit spurs this incredible couple on to greater works.

It is time for the next Great Awakening.

Bill Johnson, senior pastor of Bethel Church in Redding, California, returned home from a meeting in Toronto feeling a little disappointed at not experiencing any major manifestations or visions. The night he returned home, however, the Holy Spirit came with such power as he lay in bed that he physically shook all night long. Today Bethel is having a worldwide impact through their School of Supernatural Ministry, and they are equipping the saints to carry the message of the kingdom and God's miracle working power.[29]

Ché and Sue Ahn, Wesley and Stacey Campbell, and many other great leaders of today were also all majorly impacted by the revival in Toronto. Ché and Sue saw revival break out in Mott Auditorium, and for three years they had nightly meetings where people saw angels and experienced powerful miracles, with many coming to Christ.[30]

The miracle-working power of Jesus has begun to sweep worldwide, and Christian culture is once again shifting under the weight of a move of the Holy Spirit. The miracles continue to increase. Revivalists are moving out all over the earth, and salvation and miracles are becoming a normal part of church life once again. Revival is again breaking out in Australia and all over the world.

It is time for the next Great Awakening. I believe Paul's apostolic prayers of Ephesians 1 and 3 are being answered in our day. The Holy Spirit is enlightening the eyes of our understanding in the knowledge of Him, and the church is beginning to truly understand the riches of His glorious inheritance in the saints and the greatness of His power toward us who believe.

Imagine what it will look like to have services in which the Holy Spirit heals all who are present: paralytics all walking out of their wheelchairs, tumors disappearing or falling onto the floor, *all* the blind seeing, and *all* the deaf hearing. Everyone who reaches out to God being healed. People racing to the hospitals to bring whomever will come. The power of God being discussed in media, and the world hearing about His glory and goodness.

The church is radically awakening, yet I believe God never designed the church to simply return to the standard of the Book of Acts. He wants to do exceedingly abundantly above this. I believe that the awakening that has already begun will not only break through to the original standard but also will keep going like an enormous eruption and take the church way beyond anything we have ever dreamed of. Signs and wonders beyond anything we have ever seen will break out, and multitudes, even whole nations, will come to Christ. For the church's past pain, shame, and disgrace, there will be double recompense!

Get ready. This is going to be glorious!

WAKE UP AND REMEMBER

I've shared stories of what God is doing in the church as a whole and in the lives of individual believers. But you probably haven't been reading this book simply to enjoy the miraculous in other people's lives, have you? You want to see it in yours. How can you step into this lifestyle and live in the fullness of what God has prepared for you?

*Our response must be to ask
for rain in the time of rain.*

Remember that your faith flourishes when you are rooted and grounded in God's love for you. When you really see who He is, get a glimpse of His affection for you, and find your identity completely in His love, walking in His power becomes natural. Knowing Him intimately through the Word and through fellowship with Him, we are awakened to the destiny we have as His children. The key to a lifestyle of power is in walking in constant fellowship with the Holy Spirit. Knowing who He is and who we are in Him is the foundation we can confidently build on.

So as you root yourself in His love and rest in Him, begin to look for those who need His love. Dream with Him about what He wants to do in your life and in your world. You don't have to work your way up to a lifestyle of miracles; you are already qualified. Remember who you are in Him by setting your heart to seek His face. You are as intimately acquainted with God as you want to be.

We need to be aware of the times and seasons, and our response must be to ask for rain in the time of rain (Zech. 10:1). There is an outpouring, God is awakening His people with power, and it is time to position ourselves for more! It's time to cry out to know Him more because it is through the knowledge of Him who died for us that we discover who we are, the hope of our calling, the riches of the glory of His inheritance in the saints, and the greatness of His power toward us who believe (Eph. 1:18–19). It is only in the revelation of the light of His face that we see clearly, reflecting the character and life of the One in whose image we are made.

This is why God wants us to wake up and remember our true identity. If we are not doers of the Word, as James says, it is because we are like those who have looked into a mirror and forgotten who we are (James 1:22–25). If we are not displaying the virtues of God, it is because we have forgotten that we have been cleansed from our former sins (2 Pet. 1:8–9). God wants to remind us daily, deeply, and personally that as new creations we now have His nature and have been created for good works in Christ.

The boldness that flows from those who know they are qualified by His kindness and commissioned by His love is sparking a revolution of lovers who will declare, "Freely we have received, freely we will give." It's time to arise and join them. Let the light and glory of God be revealed in signs and wonders and miracles through you.

Notes

Introduction

1. YouTube.com, "Brisbane Miracles—God Provides a Home for the Homeless," posted by glorygathering, March 10, 2012, https://www.youtube.com/watch?v=DMybkT-r9Qg (accessed March 28, 2013).

2. James Markert, in communication with the author, November 2012. Used with permission.

Chapter 1
Understanding the Father's Heart

1. Biblesoft's *New Exhaustive Strong's Numbers and Concordance with Expanded Greek-Hebrew Dictionary*, copyright © 1994, Biblesoft and International Bible Translators, Inc.

Chapter 2
Being Transformed by His Love

1. "Amazing Grace" by John Newton. Public domain.

2. Judith Orloff, "The Health Benefit of Tears," HuffingtonPost.com, July 21, 2010, http://www.huffingtonpost.com/judith-orloff-md/emotional-wellness_b_653754.html (accessed April 1, 2013).

3. To hear a portion of a sermon I gave on this subject called "Yet You Are So Lovely," visit https://www.youtube.com/watch?v=s90Gs82BuRU (accessed April 1, 2013).

Chapter 3
Discovering the Power of Identity

1. "Because Your Grace Is Sufficient for Me" by Katherine Ruonala. Copyright Katherine Ruonala.

CHAPTER 4
FAITH ROOTED IN LOVE

1. Kathryn Kuhlman, "The Power of Love," CD.

CHAPTER 6
RESTING IN THE LORD

1. Maria Woodworth-Etter, *Signs and Wonders* (New Kensington, PA: Whitaker House, 1997), 484.
2. To view a video of Pastor Tony Thompson sharing testimonies from that series of healing meetings, visit https://www.youtube.com/watch?v=b6XXcavsY2Y (accessed April 1, 2013).
3. You can view April sharing her testimony at https://www.youtube.com/watch?v=oT1AhzuGcFs (accessed April 1, 2013).

CHAPTER 7
BUILDING ON THE ROCK

1. Smith Wigglesworth, *Ever Increasing Faith* (N.p.: Wilder Publications, 2007), 21. Viewed at Google Books.
2. E. Stanley Jones, *Mahatma Gandhi, an Interpretation* (N.p.: Abingdon-Cokesbury Press, 1948), 54; viewed at http://tera-3.ul.cs.cmu.edu/NASD/d23d381a-642a-4cb1-bd42-5373f518ed1d/lemur/2410.sgml (accessed April 2, 2013); Dibin Samuel, "Mahatma Gandhi and Christianity," ChristianToday.com, August 14, 2008, http://in.christiantoday.com/articledir/print.htm?id=2837 (accessed April 16, 2013); MKGandhi.org, "Gandhi's Message to Christians," http://www.mkgandhi.org/africaneedsgandhi/gandhi's_message_to_christians.htm (accessed April 16, 2013).

CHAPTER 11
EMBRACING GOD'S FAITHFULNESS

1. ChristianHistory.net, "John Wycliffe," August 8, 2008, http://www.christianitytoday.com/ch/131christians/moversandshakers/wycliffe.html (accessed April 3, 2013); Encyclopedia Britannica online, s.v. "John Wycliffe," http://www

.britannica.com/EBchecked/topic/650168/John-Wycliffe/8039/
Wycliffes-attack-on-the-church (accessed April 3, 2013).

2. Mark Owen, "What You Didn't Know About the Popes
of Rome," Rense.com, April 6, 2005, http://rense.com/
general63/popo.htm (accessed April 3, 2013); William J. Duiker
and Jackson J. Spielvogel, *World History: To 1800* (Indepen-
dence, KY: Cengage Learning, 2006), 393–397, as referenced in
Donna Greene, "Martin Luther's Outrage Against the Roman
Catholic Church," September 26, 2008, http://voices.yahoo
.com/martin-luthers-outrage-against-roman-catholic-1948562
.html (accessed April 3, 2013).

3. "English Bible History: The Pre Reformation History of
the Bible From 1,400 BC to 1,400 AD," http://www.greatsite
.com/timeline-english-bible-history/pre-reformation.html
(accessed April 3, 2013).

4. ChristianHistory.net, "Martin Luther," August 8, 2008,
http://www.christianitytoday.com/ch/131christians/theologians/
luther.html (accessed April 3, 2013); Encyclopedia Britannica online, s.v. "Martin Luther," http://www.britannica.com/
EBchecked/topic/351950/Martin-Luther (accessed April 3, 2013).

5. Ibid.

6. John Greenfield, *Power From on High* (N.p.: World Wide
Revival Prayer Movement, 1931), 26. Viewed at Google Books.

7. Greenfield, *Power From on High*.

8. Claude Hickman, "Count Zinzendorf," HistoryMakers
.info, http://www.historymakers.info/inspirational-christians/
count-zinzendorf.html (accessed April 3, 2013).

9. Greenfield, *Power From on High*.

10. Paul L. King, "Supernatural Physical Manifestations in
the Evangelical and Holiness Movements," paper presented at
the 32nd Society of Pentecostal Studies/Wesleyan Theological
Society Joint Conference, March 21, 2003, http://www
.pneumafoundation.org/resources/articles/manifestations.pdf
(accessed April 3, 2013).

11. ChristianHistory.net, "The Moravians and John Wesley,"
January 1, 1982, http://www.christianitytoday.com/ch/1982/
issue1/128.html (accessed April 3, 2013).

12. Greenfield, *Power From on High*.

13. Encyclopedia Britannica online, s.v. "Holiness Movement," http://www.britannica.com/EBchecked/topic/269257/Holiness-movement (accessed April 3, 2013).

14. BBC.com, "William Wilberforce," July 5, 2011, http://www.bbc.co.uk/religion/religions/christianity/people/williamwilberforce_1.shtml (accessed April 3, 2013).

15. CaneRidge.org, "Religion on America's Western Frontier," http://www.caneridge.org/history.html (accessed April 3, 2013).

16. GodsGenerals.com, "James McGready and the Kentucky Revivals," http://www.godsgenerals.com/person_james_mc.htm (accessed April 3, 2013).

17. GodsGenerals.com, "Charles Finney," http://www.godsgenerals.com/person_charles_finney.htm (accessed April 3, 2013).

18. James F. Findlay, *Dwight L. Moody: American Evangelist, 1837–1899* (Chicago: University of Chicago Press, 1969).

19. GodsGenerals.com, "Generals on God's Army," http://www.godsgenerals.com/person_w_booth.htm (accessed April 3, 2013).

20. GodsGenerals.com, "Maria Woodworth-Etter," http://www.godsgenerals.com/person_m_woodsworth-etter.htm (accessed April 3, 2013).

21. WelshRevival.com, "History," http://www.welshrevival.com/lang-en/1904history.htm (accessed April 3, 2013).

22. Revival-Library.org, "William Seymour and the History of the Azusa Street Outpouring," http://www.revival-library.org/pensketches/am_pentecostals/seymourazusa.html (accessed April 3, 2013); J. Edward Morris, Cindy McCowan, and Tom Welchel, *They Told Me Their Stories: The Youth and Children of Azusa Street Tell Their Stories* (N.p.: Dare2Dream, 2006).

23. As referenced in Pat Robertson, *Bring It On* (Nashville: Thomas Nelson, 2003), 211. Viewed at Google Books.

24. For example, see "A Revival Account Asbury 1970," *The Forerunner*, March 31, 2008, http://forerunner.com/forerunner/X0585_Asbury_Revival_1970.html (accessed April 3, 2013).

25. Andy Butcher, "Let the Multitudes Come," *Charisma*, January 31, 2001, http://www.charismamag.com/spirit/evangelism-missions/245-let-the-multitudes-come (accessed April 3, 2013).

26. Patricia L. Paddey, "Toronto Blessing Celebrates 10 Years," December 31, 2003, http://www.charismamag.com/site -archives/154-peopleevents/people-and-events/1104-toronto -blessing-celebrates-10-years (accessed April 3, 2013).

27. Marcia Ford, *Charisma Reports—the Brownsville Revival* (Lake Mary, FL: Charisma House, 1997).

28. The Remnant International, "Revival in Mozambique, Heidi and Rolland Baker," http://www.theremnant.com/11-02 -01.html (accessed April 3, 2013).

29. C. Hope Flinchbaugh, "Ignite the Fire," *Charisma*, February 28, 2007, http://www.charismamag.com/site-archives/146 -covers/cover story/2172-ignite-the-fire (accessed April 3, 2013).

30. CBN.com, "Ché Ahn: When Heaven Comes Down," April 27, 2004, http://www.cbn.com/700club/guests/bios/che_ ahn_042704.aspx (accessed March 22, 2013).

About the Author

KATHERINE RUONALA IS A prophetic revivalist who ministers both in her home base, Australia, and regularly in the United States and other nations of the world, bringing a fresh word and impartation of God's Spirit through revival services and miracle crusades. Katherine carries a strong prophetic and miracle anointing with many being instantly healed in her meetings. Reaching across denominational walls, her ministry is also used to help spread the fires of revival and ignite a fresh passion in the hearts of believers to go deeper in their relationship with God.

Katherine and Tom Ruonala are the founders and senior ministers of the international Glory City Church network (www.glorygathering.com.au). Katherine and Tom also serve as part of Harvest International Ministries Australian Apostolic team (www.harvestim.org.au), and Katherine is the founder and coordinator of the Australian Prophetic Council (http://australianpropheticcouncil.com). Katherine and Tom are happily married and have three beautiful children—Jessica, Emily, and Joseph.

To contact Katherine Ruonala Ministries,
visit www.katherineruonala.com
or e-mail invitations@katherineruonala.com.
You may also write to:

Katherine Ruonala Ministries
P. O. Box 1077
Springwood, Qld,
Australia, 4127

For information on the Glory Gathering International
Network or Glory City Church in Brisbane,
visit www.glorycitychurch.com.au.

To see our YouTube channel with video testimonies,
visit www.youtube.com/glorygathering.

To view live-streaming or archives of
Glory City Church meetings,
visit: www.livestream.com/glorycitytv.

EMPOWERED
TO RADICALLY CHANGE
YOUR WORLD

Charisma House brings you books, e-books, and other media from dynamic Spirit-filled Christians who are passionate about God.

Check out all of our releases from best-selling authors like **Jentezen Franklin**, **Perry Stone**, and **Kimberly Daniels** and experience God's supernatural power at work.

CHARISMA HOUSE

www.charismahouse.com
twitter.com/charismahouse • facebook.com/charismahouse

11843